I0836803

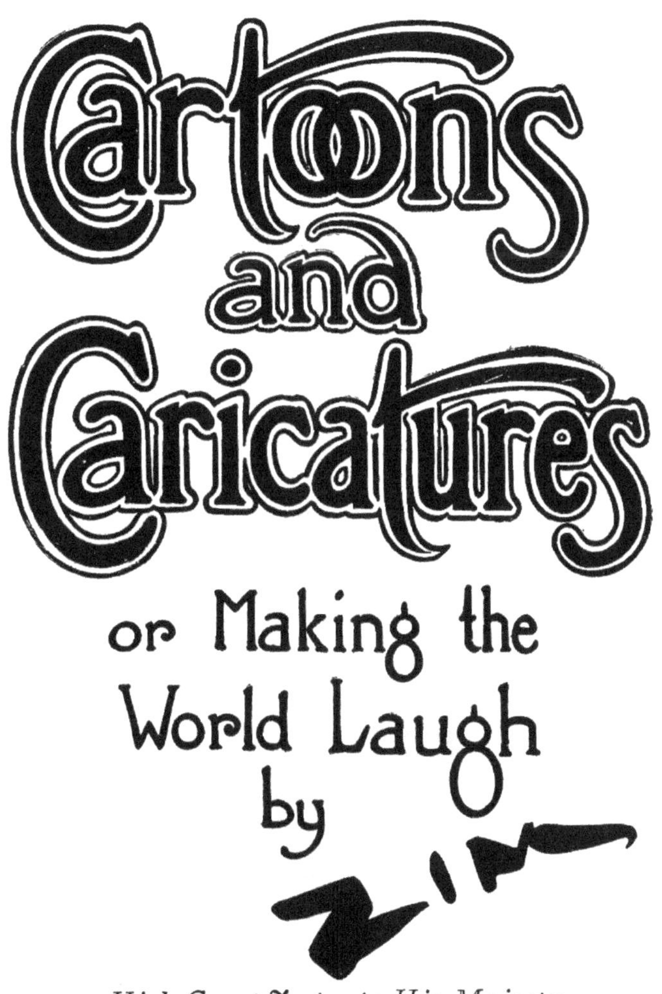

High Court Jester to His Majesty
the King of Laughter

reprinted by New York History Review
2022

Cartoons and Caricatures, or Making the World Laugh
by Eugene Zimmerman, 1910
reprinted by New York History Review, 2022

ISBN: 978-1-950822-25-6
Printed in the United States of America

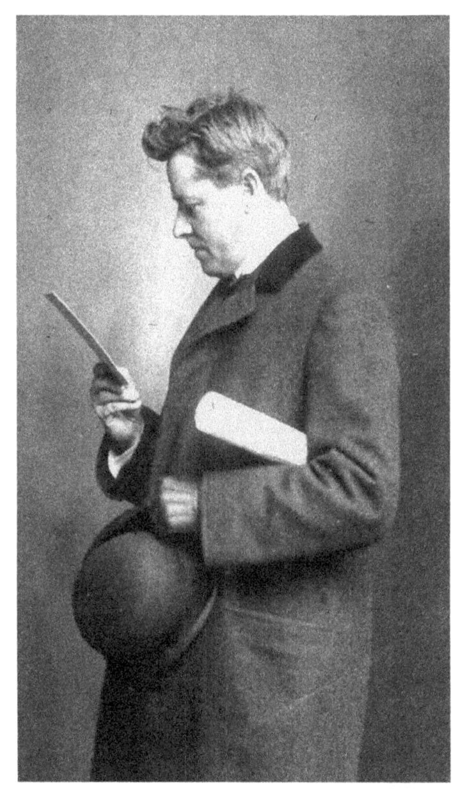

ZIM

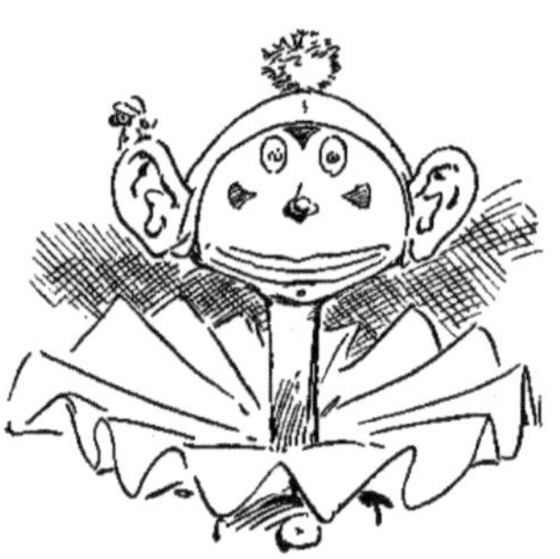

"Be Jabers!"

The ripened fruit of nearly thirty years with pen, crayon and brush, worked into a book by Eugene Zimmerman, and copyrighted by him in the archives of Washington, D. C., March, nineteen hundred and ten.

"It is to Laugh!"

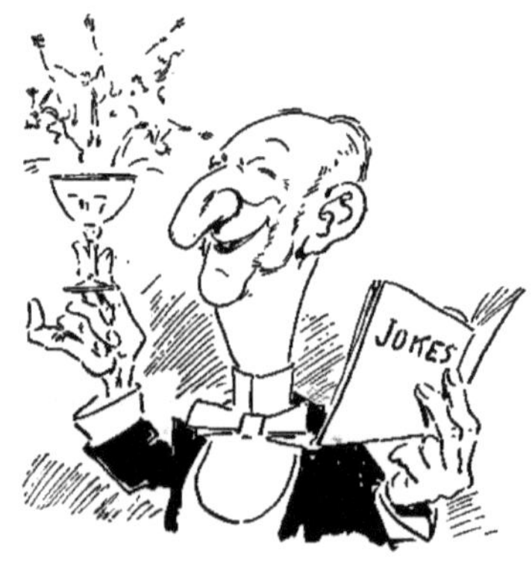

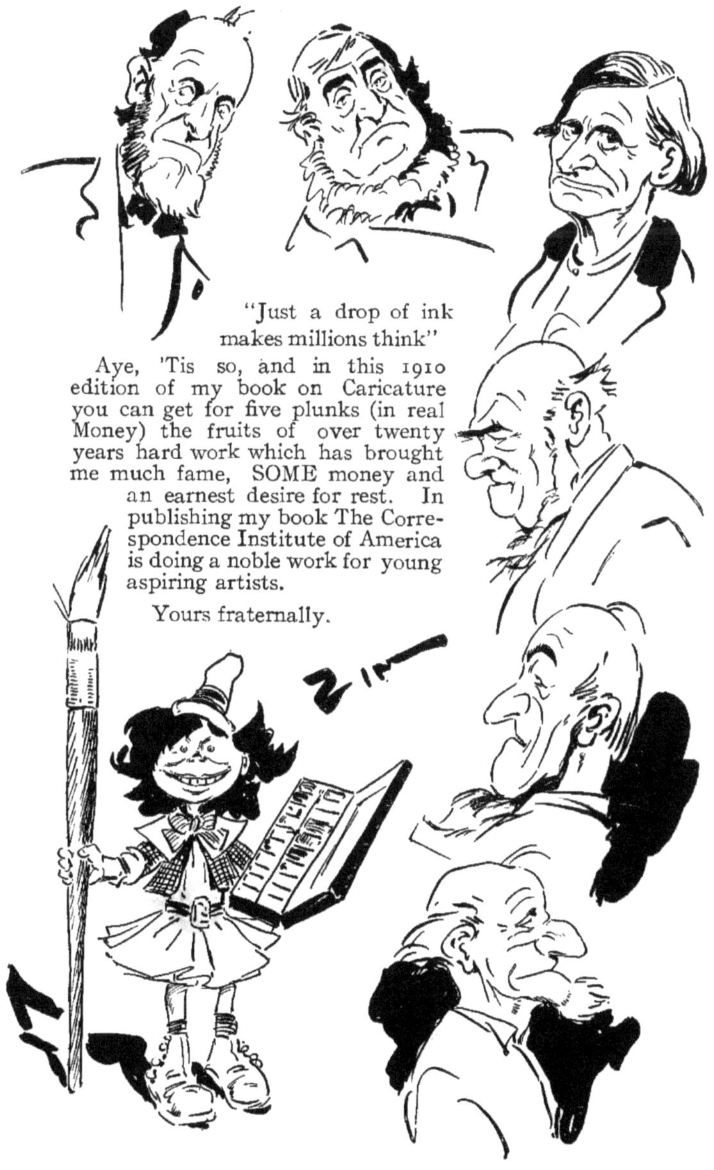

"Just a drop of ink
makes millions think"

Aye, 'Tis so, and in this 1910 edition of my book on Caricature you can get for five plunks (in real Money) the fruits of over twenty years hard work which has brought me much fame, SOME money and an earnest desire for rest. In publishing my book The Correspondence Institute of America is doing a noble work for young aspiring artists.

Yours fraternally.

Written—by fits and starts—just when I felt like it, and often when I did not—expressly for the young student bent in the direction of Comic Art and Caricature, and incidentally for the coin consideration or compensation, which a book as funny and helpful as this ought to bring.

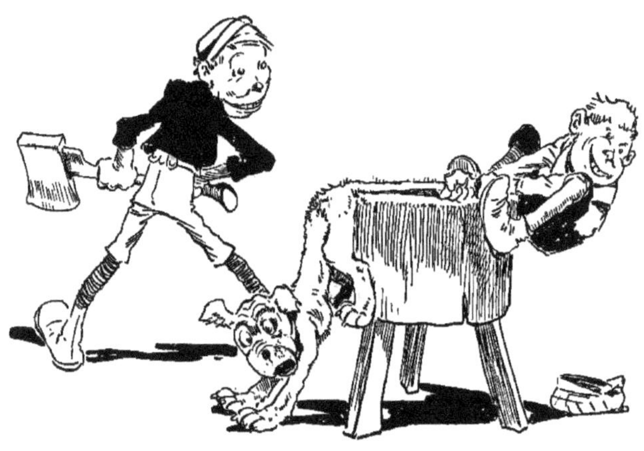

Like the works of Shakespeare, Robinson Crusoe, Burns, Byron and other men who have written some good stuff—this book is only interesting to those who are interested in it—so we'll cut the tail as short as possible.

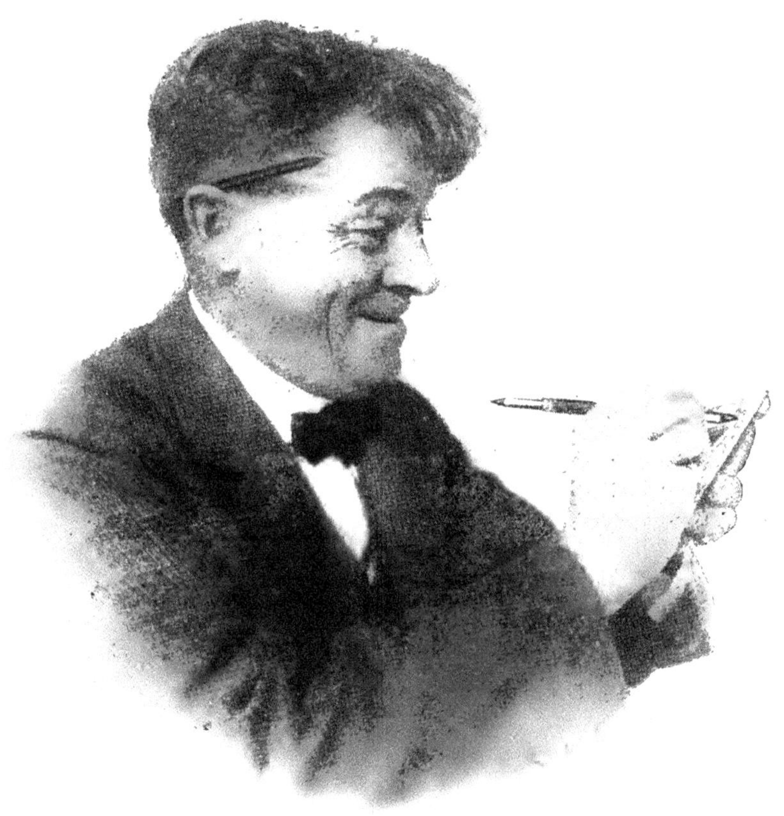

THE AUTHOR.

In Caricaturing you will note your own face gradually reflects the leading feature of the person you are sketching.

43. Married or Single
Business Lying
Early Experiences
42. This Book is Like Pumpkin Pie
41. Aches and Pains vs. Humor
40. Drawing Faces with the Aid of a Mirror
39. Cost of Line Cuts
38. The Correspondence Schools
37. Wrinkles
36. Shoes that Denote Character
35. Spatter Effects
34. Use of Scratch Board
33. The Country Post Office
32. Safest Way to Ship Drawings
31. Gestures. Drawing Expressive Hands
30. Submitting Jokes in the Rough
29. A Few Words Along Straight Lines
28. Bohemian Booze Atmosphere
Reversing a Photograph
27. Midnight Aspirations
26. Gain Friends
25. Bible Subjects and Caricatures. Captions
24. Water Color Sketch
23. Safe Transmission of Drawings
22. Wash Drawings
21. Humor and Animal Composites, and Outline of the Process of Half-tone Engraving
20. Attention to Characteristics
19. How we get Ideas
18. Spontaneity.
17. Be Modest
16. 15. The Life of a Caricaturist and the Tools he Uses
14. A Heart-to-Heart Talk
13. Practical Knowledge
12. 11. Introduction. Keyed half in fun and half in a serious vein
10. 9. 8. John Maxwell, Editor "The Home Educator," praises me while I am living. Few attain such fame and live
7. More Index
6. Index
5. My "Phiz" as it is to-day
4. How I Wrote This Book
3. An Interjection!
2. Copyright Notice
1. Title Page

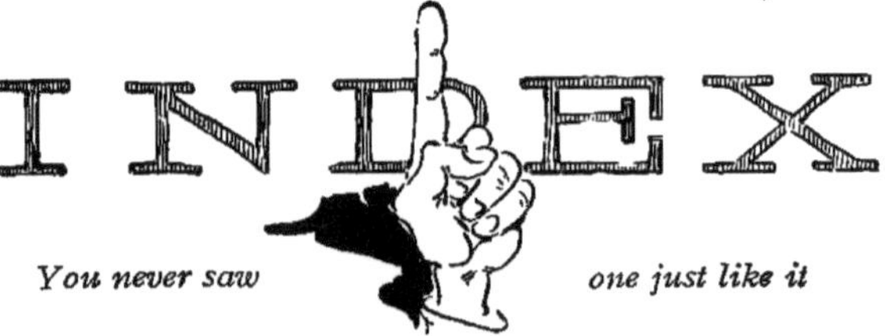

96. I say Good-bye, AND THANK YOU
95. Odd Remarks by an Odd Fellow
94. The First Great Work of my Life
93. The Man of the Hour
92. Three Commandments
91. This is a Contrary World
90. Free-lancing
89. 88. Enos. Hunter, Fisher Guide and Philosopher
87. One-sided Humor
86. The Ear and its Relation to the Face. Regarding Blacks and Whites
85. 84. Pencil and Pen Sketches
83. Nast, the Founder of American Caricature
82. Lithography
81. Gessford takes my Latest Photograph
80. History, Biography, Facts and Fibs
79. Political Cartooning
78. The Pirate
77. Two Subjects in Pen and Ink
76. Where Nature Exceeds Art
75. 74. Being your own Press Agent
73. Wash Drawings
72. Right and Wrong Interiors
71. A Few Pointers
70. The Joys of Bohemia
69. A Man's Own Castle
68. The Hobo Brand. Two Important Don'ts
67. An Illustrated Joke
66. The Affinity
65. Acrobatic Drawing
64. Drawings Based upon Puns
63. Proper Balance, and Reduction of Drawings
62. Hints on Practice
61. Don't Waste your Genius
60. Companion Pictures
59. Character Sketch
58. Don't Be Too Nervy
57. Blacks and Whites
56. The Prolific Man
55. Drawing a Sketch on Common Packing Board
54. Nearly a Soljer
53. Good Advice
52. Ideas in the Rough
51. Comic Sketch
50. Sketch on Charcoal Board
49. Drawing up an Idea
48. The Artist and the Art Editor
47. Sample of Finished Pen Sketch
46. What's in a Name
45. The Caricaturist as a Hero
44. Study the Comic Journals

EUGENE ZIMMERMAN

CARTOONIST

Known the World Over as "Zim"

An Appreciation by John Maxwell, Editor "The Home Educator"

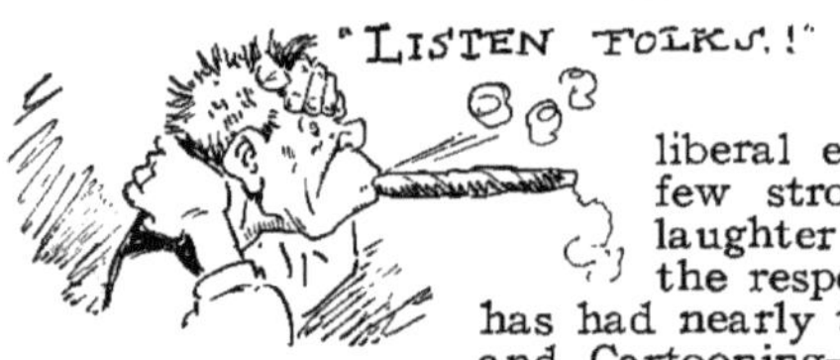

TO know Eugene Zimmerman is to love him; to study his work is a liberal education in the power of a few strokes of the pen to create laughter and at the same time hold the respect of all interested. "Zim" has had nearly thirty years in Caricaturing and Cartooning—a longer actual art career than any other living Cartoonist. He takes his work as his Life's work—to do things well he says is a serious thing—a duty we owe to ourselves and our friends, the public. Yet "Zim" as a man is bubbling over with humor. He's a jolly character—a man among men—King of Cartoonists and Prince of Caricaturists. He, among our great artists of to-day, is credited with having the greatest amount of humor; is well known in all circles of Bohemia and Art—yet, loves the hours best that he spends in Chemung county, New York. When I first approached him regarding his new book, "Cartoons and Caricatures, or, Making the World Laugh," I found him, the Artist in his Studio on Fifth avenue, New York. Later when I was commissioned to get "Zim" to thoroughly revise the Art Course of the Correspondence Institute of America, I found him a man of leisure amid the thousand and one artistic creations of his retreat in upper New York State. In both cases he took life easy, for he feels he deserves to do so and the one great charm about him is his cheery optimism. "Laugh and the world laughs with you," seems to be his motto, and yet he has had his ups and downs. He is forty years young—as genial as a school-boy, happy as a man always is who loves his work—fatherly in his advice—brotherly in his big-hearted friendship for those who admire him—and he has thousands of admirers. Just the kind of a comrade to warm up to—a true artist and a good citizen. When you take into consideration the reputation artists as a rule enjoy for being erratic, it means a lot when I say Eugene Zimmerman has always been a leading cartoonist in political campaigns for the past thirty years and has never been defiled by taint of party politics or plunder and the wealth he enjoys has been the legitimate proceeds of his art. He is a Swiss, having been born in Basle, May 25th, 1862, and two years later, upon the death of his mother, he was sent to live with an aunt in Alsace until the outbreak of the Franco-Prussian war in 1870. The din of war and the clash of strife sunk deep into his youthful nature and he loves to dash sketches of what he thinks they ought to have let him do to cool his martial ardor. (These and nearly one hundred of his sketches appear in the Art Course of the C. I. of A.) The war had just started when they shipped "Zim" in care of a friend to join his father, a baker in Paterson, N. J. He attended the public schools of that city and received much chastising for drawing pictures on his slate, on the blackboards and in his school books. He asserts his work was not popular with his teachers. He drifted into this and that, and his life story reads like a dime novel, only truth in this case is stranger than fiction. Between the years of 15 and 22, "Zim" tells me he was a star actor on Life's Stage and played many parts—tragic and otherwise: He was a farmer's chore boy, assistant peddler of fish, a baker, attended bar, a sign writer, a painter upon fences, and a whitewasher of fences, a worker in a silk mill, odd man on a farm; with brief intervals between each engagement and his resignation was accepted at all times, for he believed he was cut out for but one career—that of a newspaper artist. His mind was on one subject and in cultivating his artistic talent he undoubtedly neglected at times the duties he was supposed to attend to. He says he endured many hardships but he never despaired of being some day a cartoonist. He really broke into art by becoming a sign painter in New York City. "Zim" admits his signs attracted attention. "They were funny," is the way he summed them up, and judging them by his sketches I quite believe they were. While working on signs, some of his work came to the attention of the proprietors of "Puck," and he joined them in 1884, when he was but 22 years of age. He served out his three years' contract and joined "Judge," and he has been for the past 23 years the great caricaturist of the well-known and world-read publication. His humor is delicate and refined. What Eugene Field was to the poetical world, Eugene Zimmerman is to the world of caricature and humor. Some people laugh with their face—others with their whole body—"Zim's" pictures make you laugh all over. He admits from the depth of his wisdom that seventy per cent of those we meet talk with their hands —and "Zim" draws hands and feet—gestures and facial expressions—wrinkles and curves—a dash here and a dot there, as no other cartoonist ever did, and I am pleased to say he has incorporated in the thirty revised lessons of the Art Course of the Correspondence Institute of America, some of his sketches specially drawn as aids to the young student in Illustrating, Designing and Cartooning. "Zim" stands without a rival in his field; no cartoonist can show so much with so few dashes of a pen; he seems niggardly with his lines, yet he is most prodigal in the humor he serves up to us.

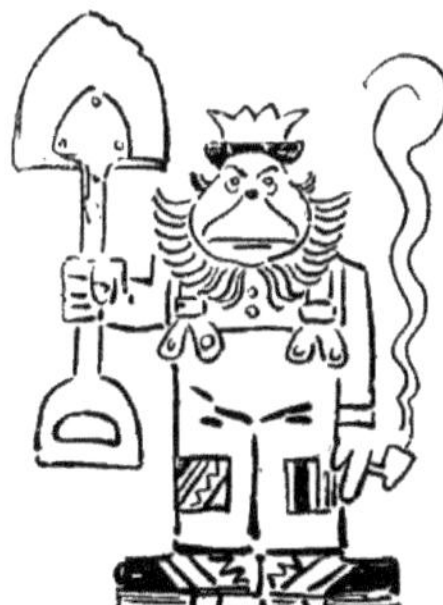

There are many cartoonists and comic artists—many good men with their heart in their work; men I have had the pleasure of meeting during the past fifteen years—men who are real creators—artists who have established the serial drawings, appearing in all the Sunday editions of our metropolitan papers—that create laughter, interest and humor. But who among the vast army of comic artists and cartoonists can in any measure equal "Zim?" Who besides "Zim" can draw a real hand, a real foot, or a smile upon the face and still make it funny? There are none! "Zim" is in a world by himself, surrounded by a million admirers, who eagerly await each week the welcomed copy of "Judge," wherein appear "Zim's" refreshing and refined fountains of mirth, happiness and laughter, at the waters of which we may drink abundantly and drive away the cares of a weary brain, and renew the sunshine of happiness. "Zim's" drawings have a literary finish, an artistic appreciation, and to these he always adds a sprinkling of refined and delicate humor.

We as an American people, lovers of refined, delicious humor and funny drawings, must all humbly bow at the shrine of Eugene Zimmerman, who has no equal, therefore no superior in the broad field of his fine humor and comedy sketching.

If Byron were living, I believe he would repeat these words in due reverence to "Zim:"

"Dreams in their development have breath,
And tears and tortures, and the touch of joy."

Eugene Zimmerman is a great man, a great thinker, a great creator and master of originality; the one man who compels millions to laugh. As I have said before, to see him would be to love him—love him because of his genial and sunny disposition; the shake of his hand is a true symbol of loyalty and good, true fellowship.

To be in his presence is to be in the atmosphere of happiness, where care is unknown and trouble a stranger. He loves his work; he loves to make othere happy, and the latch string of his heart always hangs out to those who need help, cheer and consolation. May the good fellowship of love always be his, and may he ever be prosperous and happy in this hard world of strife and trouble.

As a parting toast in behalf of all those who admire him, who enjoy his soft flow of delicious humor and his funny sketches, I cannot do better than to quote Eugene Field, and apply to "Zim" a toast from us all:

"Here's to you, 'Zim,'
May you live one thousand years
To sort'er keep things lively,
In this vale of human tears.
And here's that we may live
One thousand years, too,
Did I say a 'thousand years?'
No, a thousand less a day;
For I should hate to live on earth,
And learn that you had passed away."

John Maxwell.

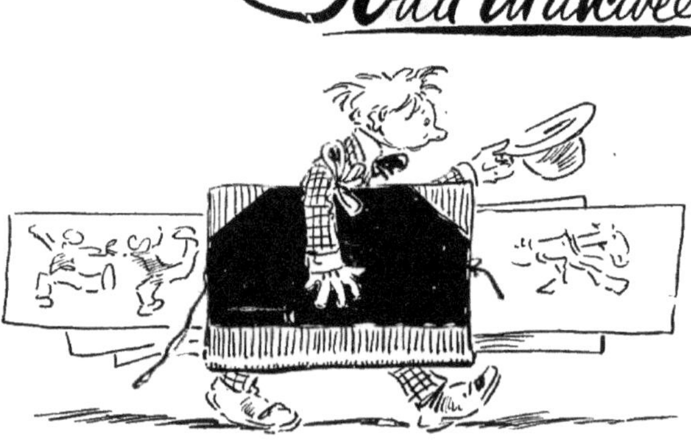

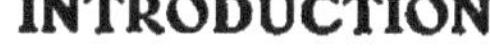

INTRODUCTION

FAME brings its glories and its trials. I constantly receive letters asking for "straight tips" how to win out in the Pictorial field. My spirit is willing, but the flesh is weak; I cannot attempt to answer the thousand and one questions put to me by kindly correspondents, so I do the next best thing. I give you in these pages the concentrated essence of nearly thirty years of experience as a Cartoonist making the world laugh. I write more or less haphazard—just as the thoughts come to me—a book of instruction that will, I know, appeal to the young student of both sexes who lack opportunities for personal contact with men of experience, and by whom an Art Education would be difficult were it not for the excellent method laid down in the Course for Home Study put out by the Correspondence Institute of America, Scranton, Pa.

Nearly thirty years with the pen, crayon and brush makes me one of the "Old Guard," and although an appreciative public has placed me among the leaders, I can never forget my early struggles, and I want, indeed, I earnestly desire to help on the young student because I want him to LOVE HIS WORK as I have loved it, and that WITH APPLICATION is the true secret of Success.

After long years in Comic Art, Cartooning and Caricaturing, I give you in pure but simple language, remarks with humorous illustrations which will point the way to a good, and I know an honest living, for laughter does more for the world than much of its misdirected energy in a dozen ways. Technical terms I cut out, I do not want to confuse you, as you go on you will absorb them easily enough. Neither do I in the instructions I give you deal with tonsorial art, fancy gardening, or artistic horse-shoeing, nor any other cult with which I am not familiar. Caricature I am thoroughly familiar with, and with that through these pages you and I will journey—loaf by the wayside for a breathing spell at times, then go on, and I trust reach our journey's end with both pleasure and profit.

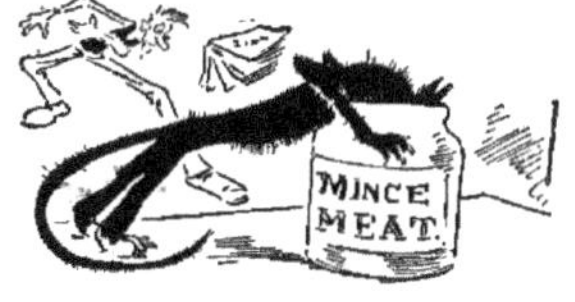

I really don't think the dear Lord ever intended that I should write a book. I was driven to it, however, to satisfy the laudable craving for information in the art direction of their talents that all young and aspiring artists (especially those of

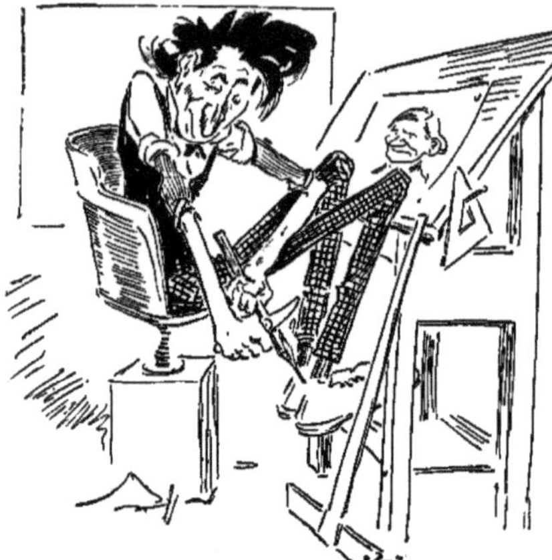

moderate means and away from art centers) possess.

You can read and profit by my experience. I am basking to-day in the sunshine which a well-spent, hard-worked life brings, but I have gone through, taken all degrees and graduated from the School of Hard Knocks and profited by the buffettings of Fate.

My sketches will I trust, help to make the reading less tedious, and the two combined will serve to throw at the cat when ever she sticks her nose nto your business.

ALWAYS SMILE—then smile again—then keep on smiling. It's the finest tonic known. I know it! ALWAYS FACE THE SUN!

"Don't hunt after trouble, but look for success,
You'll find what you look for; don't look for distress.
If you see but your shadow, remember, I pray,
That the sun is still shining, but you're in the way.
Don't grumble, don't bluster, don't dream and don't shirk,
Don't think of your worries, but think of your work.
The worries will vanish, the work will be done,
No man sees his shadow who faces the sun."

DON'T BACK-PEDAL. Keep on, and in keeping on you will go upward!

Life isn't all sunshine. We wouldn't appreciate the sun if clouds did not arise now and again.

DON'T WHINE. Thousands of people in small positions whine because their ability has no elbow-room. It is not elbow-room they need; it is "ELBOW-GREASE;" it is energy and strength. Their very whining shows they are too small for the place they are in now. When the right kind of a person has too small a place he does his work so well as to make the the place bigger. Let's get in and make the job bigger, and in making the job bigger we get bigger, and the world gets our best. My little talk written in a varying tone of seriousness and humor is nearly done.

I've had a lot to do with publishers, and if you go on and win you will have too, so here's a little joke for you to illustrate later on: He was a newspaper publisher and lay ill. The doctor came, put his ear to his breast and said, "All that troubles you, my dear sir, is that your circulation is bad."

"Circulation bad, Doctor?" shrieked the man as he shot upright in his bed, "Why, man, we have the largest circulation in the State!"

Yours for success,

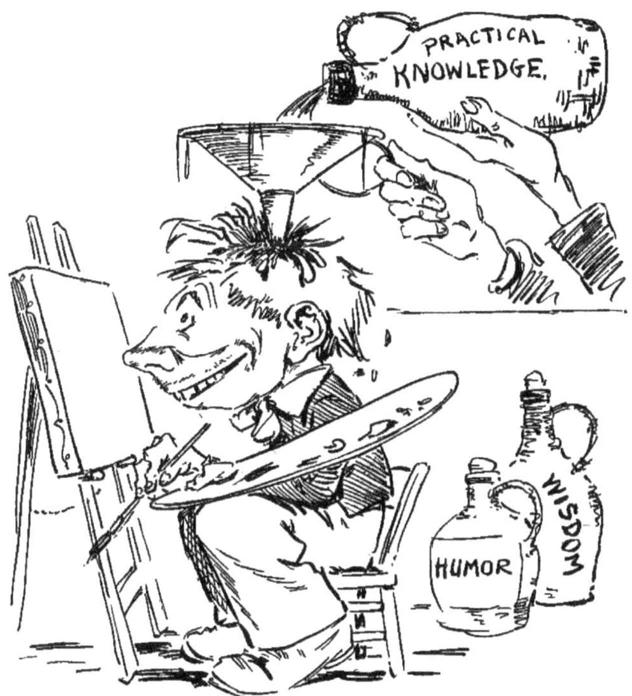

YOUNG man, before you start out on your wild and checkered career, permit me to spill a few valuable notions into your head.

In the first place try to forget that you are a great artist: And lead a natural life. Don't be too eccentric. Be like other poor mortals who love to earn an honest living, and the world will love you the better for it.

When you get into the public eye you have opened the way for innocent attacks upon your good name. For instance, many families in the middle and lower walks of life deem it an honor to name their last born after you. Others feel privileged in calling their pet pugs after you. This much you can tolerate, but when the village cigar maker insists upon placing your cherished name on his latest five cent production, you begin to wish that Destiny had been less kind to you. This is what happened to me, and it fell to my lot to make a label to fit the weed, a sample copy being first presented to me from which to draw my inspiration. Let my fate be a warning to fond mothers whose talented sons are forging to the front.

A ♥ TO ♥ TALK

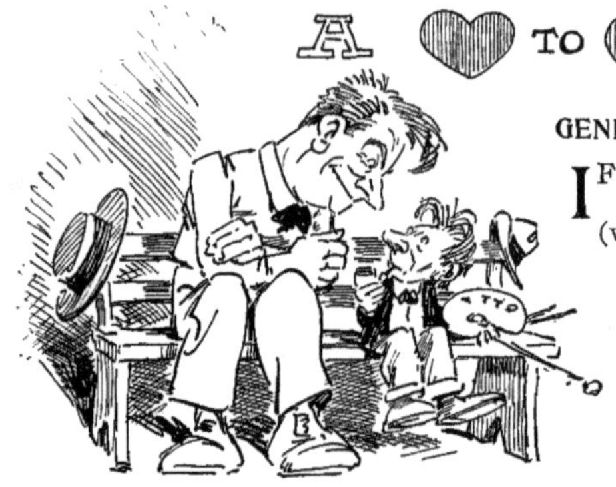

GENIUS vs. BUSINESS ABILITY

IF you feel at all discontented with your lot (which is more than likely, for most artists do), just make a careful observation of the surrounding situation, and take the following into consideration. You are young and have genius, which is always in demand, and will compensate you when fully developed. Your only investment is your brain.

The business man may have superior business ability, but he must first invest a sum of money in order to make money. He may invest in mortgages at six per cent. interest, or in merchandise which in time will pay him a profit. Suppose you earn $100 a week at drawing pictures without the investment of a dollar, all clear profit, as it were, the business man may be obliged to carry a stock of from five to twenty thousand dollars to gain a profit of $100 per week. He has also rent and clerks to pay, insurance on his stock, etc. So then, don't you think you should feel contented even at $25 per week if the work is steady and if you are not too anxious to possess automobiles and other luxuries?

PREVAILING COMPLAINTS OF STUDENTS

The prevailing complaint of the student is that he doesn't progress as fast as he would like, that his instructor will give him nothing but simple subjects to draw, such as lines and cross-hatching. Suppose you sought a position in a bank, would you not prefer to commence at the bottom and gradually work up to the presidency?

Get the proper swing first, just like a child learns music, learn to run the scale, as it were, before you tackle Beethoven. Your instructor is not blind to your faults and in a methodical way is helping you to overcome them.

Your head is like an incandescent lamp, your brain like the carbon. Regulate your lamp of genius with the incandescent in your bed chamber. When you turn the button the light goes to sleep until summoned again. Let that be your motto—when the light goes out, go to sleep; get good, refreshing sleep, and start in with a clear mind in the morning, and ideas will come to you fast and plenty.

Napoleon Bonaparte was a great thinker. He said (according to historians) that his head was like a bureau—full of drawers. Each drawer contained certain thoughts. When he retired he locked all the drawers and went peacefully to sleep. You can do likewise if you'll exert your will power

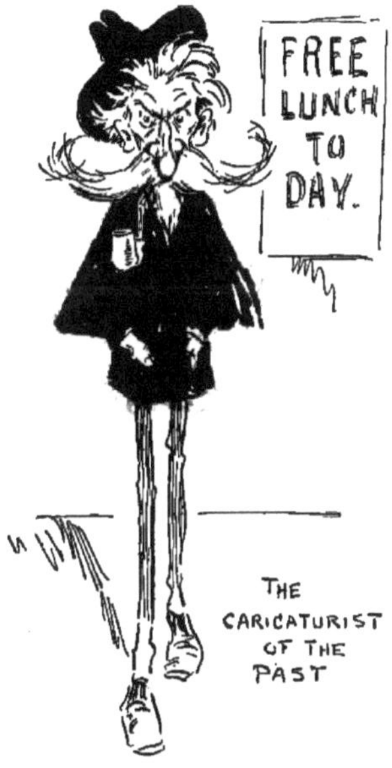

THE CARICATURIST OF THE PAST

THE LIFE OF THE CARICATURIST

THE life of the caricaturist is much the same as the life of the proverbial plumber—both command large salaries.

The caricaturist must have a keen perception of right and wrong, but not so keen that he can detect the political faults of his own party. He represents the only party of purity and reform. In the opposition he must see nothing but corruption and mismanagement—for this he is paid a good round salary. The more fault he can find with his political rivals, the LARGER and *"rounder"* his salary becomes. The caricaturist has opinions of his own, but they may easily be remoulded by an offer of a more lucrative position on a newspaper of opposite political faith, whereupon he immediately sees the unpardonable crimes and corruption of the party he has just deserted.

When caricature was in its infancy, the man known to the world as a caricaturist was looked upon as a wonder. He had no predecessors to inspire him; he worked alone and without any of the facilities which we enjoy in the present day. Science has bestowed upon us new methods of engraving so simple that it requires only a few hours to produce results that would have occupied days or weeks in times of wood engraving.

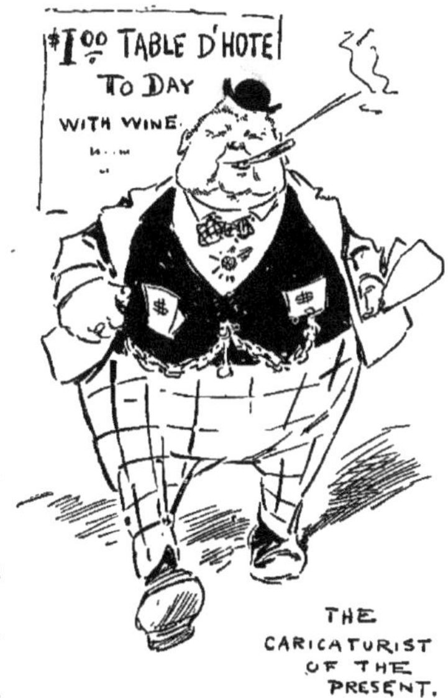

THE CARICATURIST OF THE PRESENT.

Caricaturing is a pleasant vocation now-a-days, especially if there is a substantial salary attached to it You may take your profession with you anywhere, and gather material wherever you happen to be.

The main point in the profession is "The Lead Pencil"

How to carve it, and other advice to the unsophisticated.

WHENEVER You sketch in

"HERE'S THE POINT"

public, in order to throw your audience off the track and make them think that you are a full-fledged caricaturist, always wear a reckless air and a common twenty-five cent necktie.

Sharpen your pencil as though it was born in you. In doing so be careful to use a jack-knife. The style of pencils mostly used by the profession cost about nine cents per dozen net and about twelve cents per dozen minus the net. They are the product of a Jersey lead mine and run in strata like the formation of the earth. The surface pans about 95 per cent. pure lead, gradually running into a bed of clay, now and then striking a vein of quicksand, and a "bum" rubber on the end constitutes the lead pencil.

INDIA INK

If any man expects a bigger layout of real estate for the amount invested, he is not worthy of a place among us.

However, while you are starting out to master the art, you may as well start right. Get the best quality of pencils in the market, F. W. Faber's or Dixon's, for instance. If you use good material and good tools, you will feel better satisfied with your work.

A good pen is the only pen fit to use. I find it easier to draw a good picture with a good pen than to draw a poor picture with a poor pen. The pens that have given the best satisfaction in my kind of work are as follows:

Gillott's No. 290 for fine work on faces.

Gillott's No. 303 for ordinary rough work, and Gillott's No. 659 Crowquill.

Each of these I use alternately. Whenever I find one acting balky I retire it and try another.

SPONGE RUBBER

Condition of Tools

Keep your working material and tools clean and in good order. If you allow yourself to become careless in this respect your drawings will show the effects of your negligence. A sheet of tracing paper should be included in your outfit. To make it, take any ordinary thin linen paper and sprinkle a bit of dry Prussian blue upon one side and rub it thoroughly with a cloth. One sheet will last a year and proves very handy in tracing your sketch upon clean cardboard, if you do not wish to work directly upon it with lead pencil.

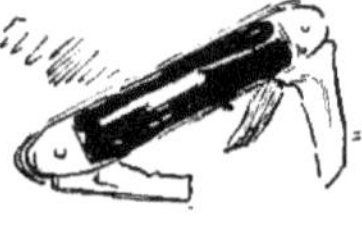

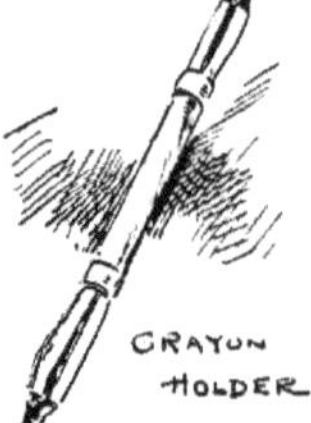

CRAYON HOLDER

BE MODEST

TO be successful as a funny man you should be unassuming. Don't presume to know it all, and by all means do not force your efforts upon the public and point to yourself as the real thing. Side-splitting jokes and sketches are usually created in seclusion, and not in the midst of an admiring crowd showering praises upon you.

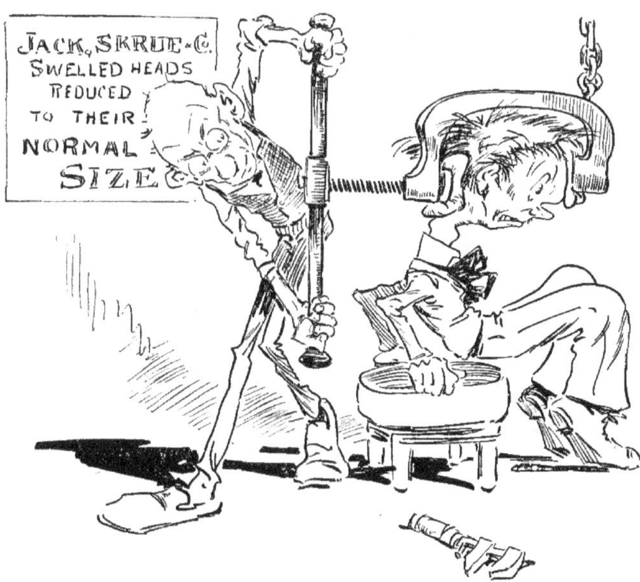

Don't allow your head to get swelled by flattery. Measure your own importance and use common sense in doing so. Take success modestly and don't go 'round telling people you had a picture published last week—it is more gratifying to have them remind you that they saw your picture in print. And should your drawings be returned marked "not available," don't despair, but slam right in and produce more and of better quality, if possible. When once you have made a "hit" the publishers will ask for your entire output, together with those rejected drawings of former days.

Don't ask silly questions such as, "How do you like my style of drawing?" or "Don't you think I'm improving?" Modesty compels the interrogated party to say, "Yes; it is great!" etc., when down deep in his soul he thinks you're a *Homarus Vulgaris.*

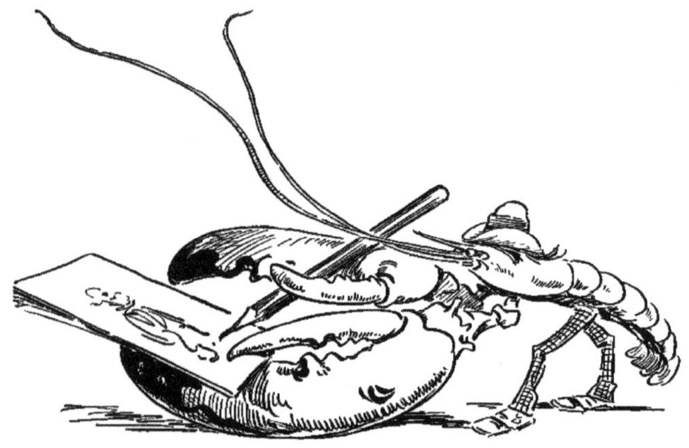

A "HOMARUS VULGARIS"

SPONTANEITY

To illustrate to you how easily ideas come to one when one is on the alert for them. Some time ago I purchased a 15 cent package of silver enamel, which was accompanied by a booklet informing the good and economical housewife how to daub it on to make everything look like new. I was at the same time breaking my head over an idea for a double page for "Judge," which I must get out at once. On reading the instructions in said booklet I struck the exact idea that I wanted. Well, you wouldn't believe it, but that 15 cent package was the best investment I ever made.

Though I am interested in all sorts of Get Broke Quick Concerns, that was the first and only time I ever got my original capital out of any silver or gold investment.

HOW DO WE GET OUR IDEAS?

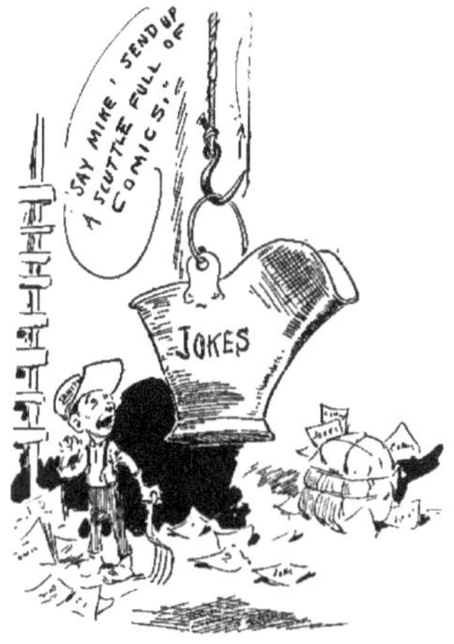

WELL, they come to us in various ways. A caricaturist as a rule relies principally upon his own fertile brain for his material. When his resources become exhausted, which is often the case, then he resorts to ideas which may come in the mail from outside contributors, or suggestions from friends. He sees many way out of his predicament, as his mind is so thoroughly trained he can cope with any emergency. Every artist has more or less of the so-called emergency material on hand in the rough state. He turns to this, when occasion demands.

"ALL YOU NEED TO SAY"

but enclose stamps for a reply.

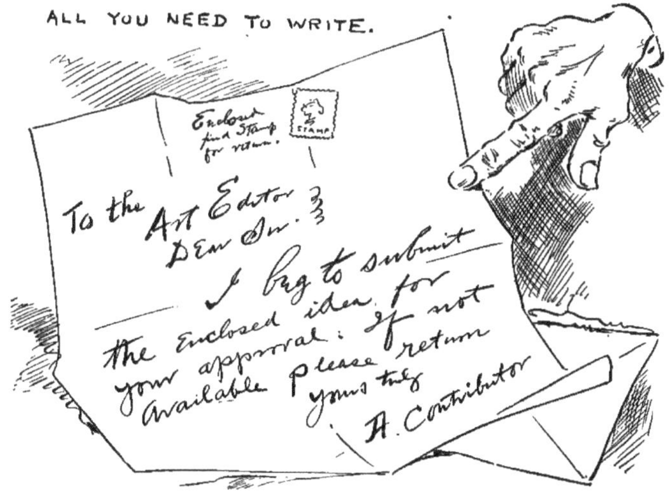

ATTENTION TO CHARACTERISTICS

SUPPOSE your subject is a man with decided features. You first observe in his face the characteristic lines. If his nose is inclined to be chubby, then increase its chubbiness a trifle. If it inclines toward the long, lean hook nose, then add a bit to the hook and length. Not enough, however, to lose the resemblance to the original. A high or low forehead you must increase or diminish as the case may call for. Thus you go through the entire body, legs and feet, giving to each member its characteristic peculiarity. If your subject possesses a wart on the tip of the nose or elsewhere in sight, then it also belongs there in the picture; but don't make those unnatural growths too disgustingly conspicuous. When possible avoid such offensive adjuncts as warts, corns, bunions, club feet, mutilated hands or anything that is liable to retard the fun in your pictures.

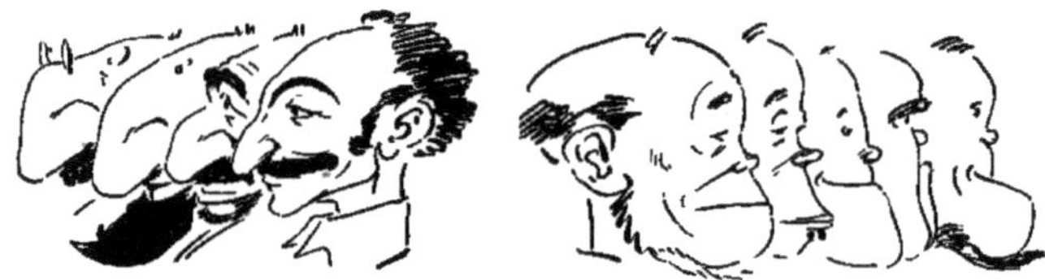

Take for example the Hebrew and the Irish face as the two extremes for characteristic curves. You already know that to produce an Irish face you must give it a pug nose, and the Hebrew face the hook nose, though these essentials in drawing do not always exist in nature. I have seen Irishmen with decided Jewish noses, and Jews with noses a little inclined the other way. However, to carry out the purpose of your picture you must stick to these characteristics.

HUMAN AND ANIMAL COMPOSITES

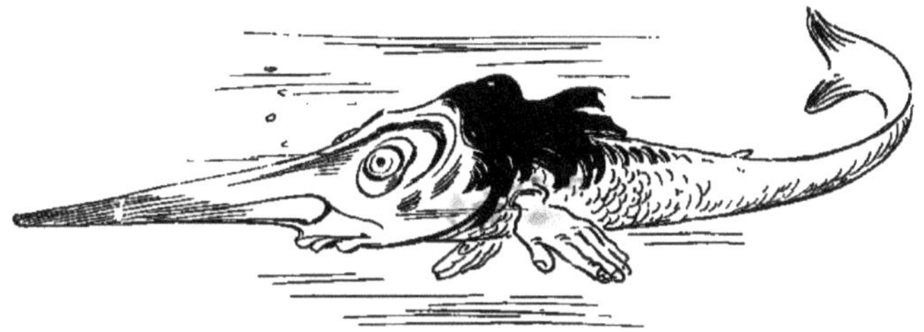

IT IS part of the caricaturist's business to see things as they are not. For instance, in transforming a human face into that of an animal, the artist observes the expressive lines of the human face and those of the animal. He then proceeds to amalgamate the two, being careful to retain the original likeness.

AN OUTLINE OF THE PROCESS OF HALF-TONE ENGRAVING

The methods employed in producing a half-tone cut are rather complicated and somewhat difficult to describe. In the first place, the drawing (wash drawing) is photographed on to a negative, the negative is developed and dried. Then it is placed over a sensitized copper plate with another glass with lines on it, which is called a screen, placed between the negative and copper plate. The combination fastened in a frame is then placed in a strong light, the light affecting the sensitized plate in the same manner as other photographs are printed. The copper plate is then placed in a bath of acid for a short period. This is called etching. When the plate is sufficiently etched it is washed and mounted on a block of wood and is then ready for the printer.

The only difference between half-tone and line cut engraving is the introduction of the glass screen, which has on its surface many very fine black lines. The finest screen used for magazine work contains about 150 lines to the inch; making the cost about double.

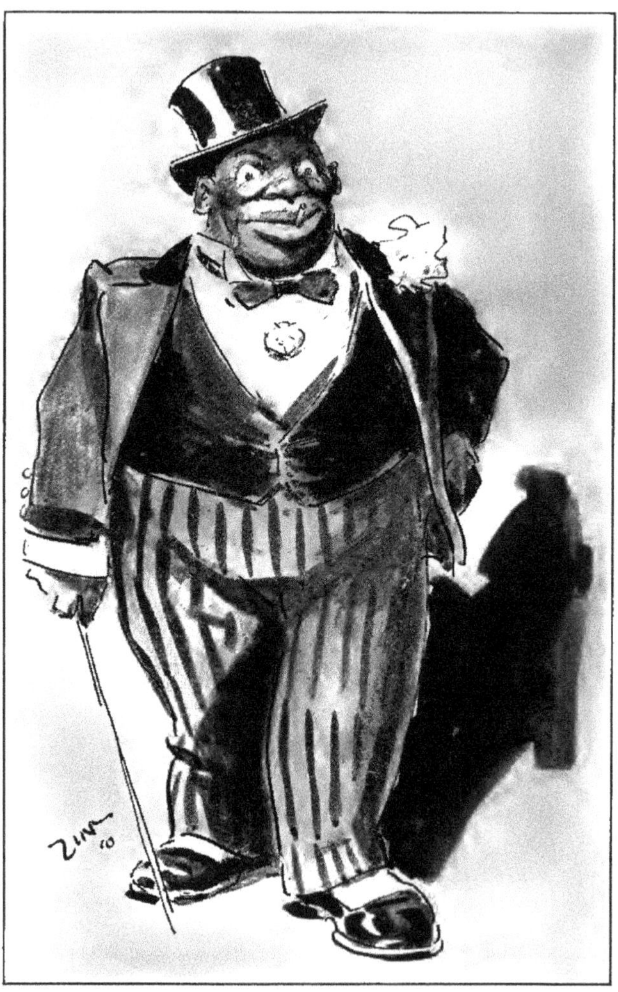

WASH DRAWING;

as prepared for half-tone plate. The engraver should pay careful attention to hand tooling the white portion, such as shirt, cuffs, collar and spats.

SAFE TRANSMISSION OF DRAWINGS

(See also page 28)

TO prevent drawings from being jammed or broken in the mail, enclose them in cardboard tubes or between heavy sheets of pasteboard. The publishers will not be responsible for any neglect on your part in preparing them for safe transmission.

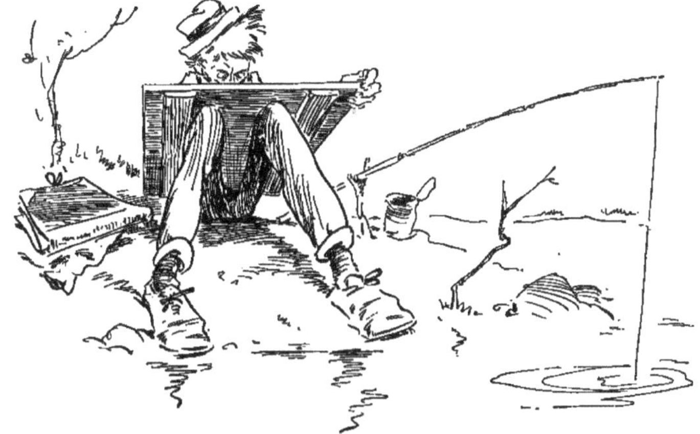

COMBINING BUSINESS WITH PLEASURE

Fishing is splendid recreation for head-workers. In my opinion, all head-workers ought to fish at least a full ten hours each day and sleep the rest of the time. This rule followed 365 days in the year will be found very quieting to the nervous system.

I am sure I have made an error in the title of this book. It should read, "First Aid to the Afflicted."

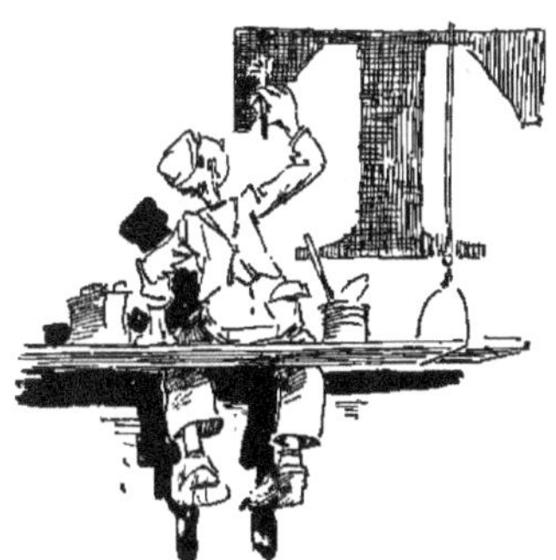

HE sign painting trade seems to have played a prominent rôle in the lives of men who have achieved fame in art and literature. There seems to be a sort of relationship between sign writing and comic art. There is no denying the fact that one, in order to be a good newspaper artist, should know something about lettering, for in many instances you will be called upon to make suitable headings for stories and special column headlines. If you have ever had experience as a sign writer you will, no doubt, realize this fact.

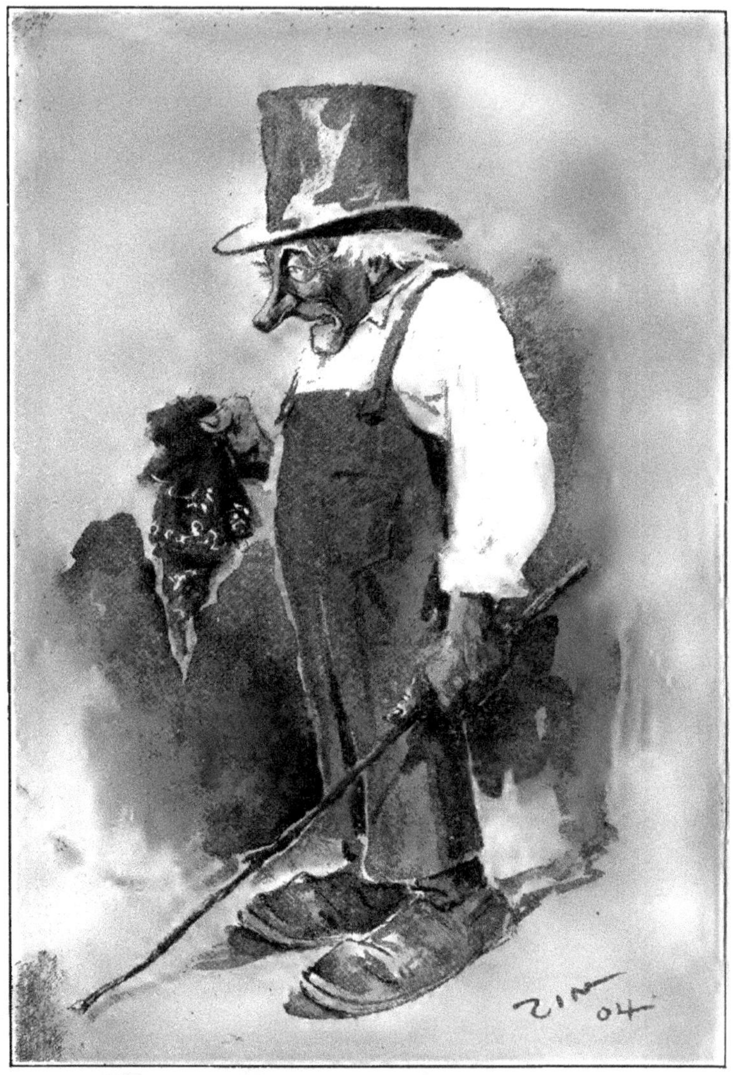

PLATE MADE FROM WATER COLOR SKETCH. SIZE OF ORIGINAL, 15X20 INCHES. THIS STYLE OF PLATE IS CALLED "HALF-TONE"

BIBLE SUBJECTS AND CARICATURE

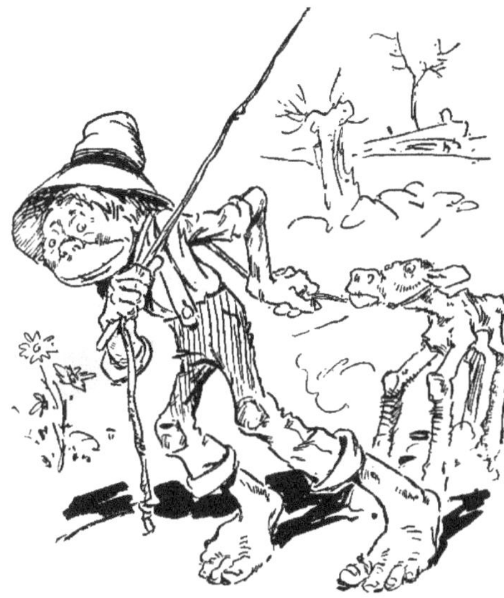

A STUBBORN PROPOSITION

SACRILEGIOUS application of Biblical subjects to fit political situations should not be attempted. It is bad form to link the name of the Saviour with that of the politician.

The more you boil down sap the richer will be your syrup. Likewise with a caption, the briefer the caption, the better the joke.

CAPTIONS

"Captions in vernacular," means the reading matter below the picture, written in the language of any particular locality, without regard to grammar. Every city has its East or West side, where a certain class exists who talk any way but correctly.

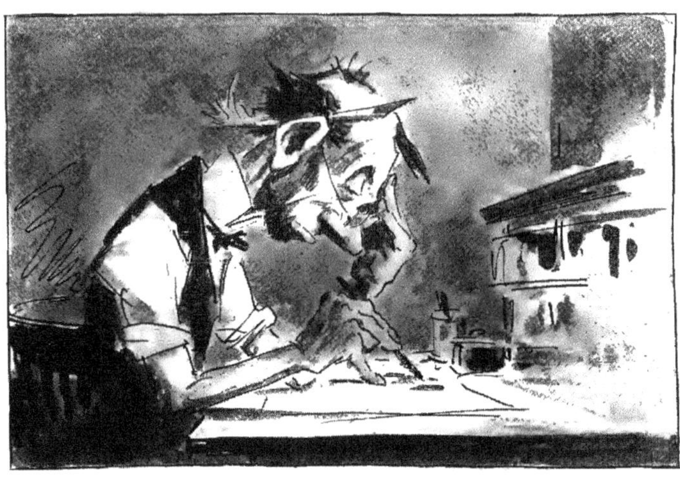

A COUNTRY EDITOR WITH HIS "NOSE ON THE GRINDSTONE"

GAIN FRIENDS

IT is cowardly and in very bad taste to caricature deformities when it affects an individual, either in public or private life. The sympathy of your audience will naturally lean in the direction of your unfortunate subject and affect their appreciation of your genius. In ordinary comics which bear no likeness to anyone in particular, you may take such liberties, so long as you do not carry them to the point of hideousness.

Aim to make your pictures pleasing, not repulsive; thereby making friends not enemies—for upon the merits of your work depends your success.

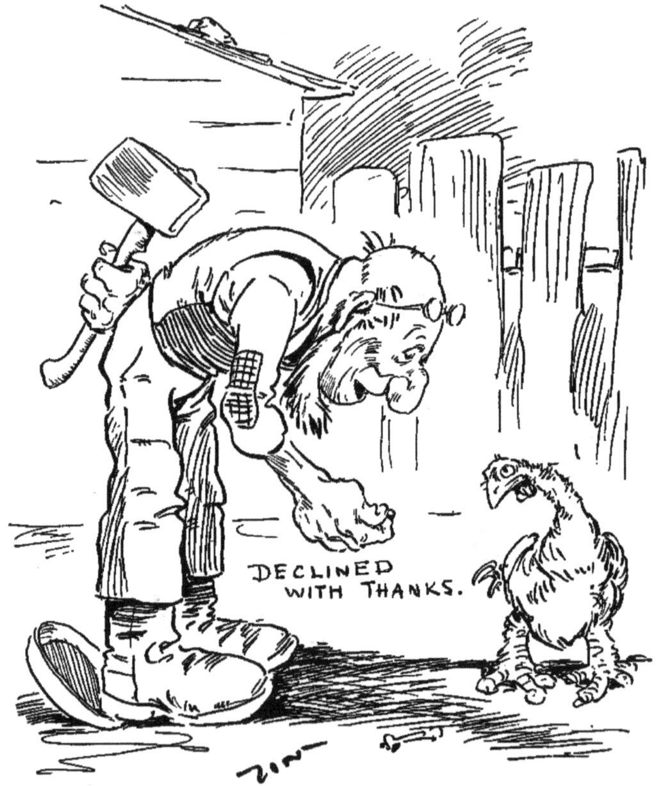

Suspicious Old Hen: "I see the point! I eat with you to-day and you eat with me to-morrow. A sort of reciprocity."

MIDNIGHT INSPIRATIONS

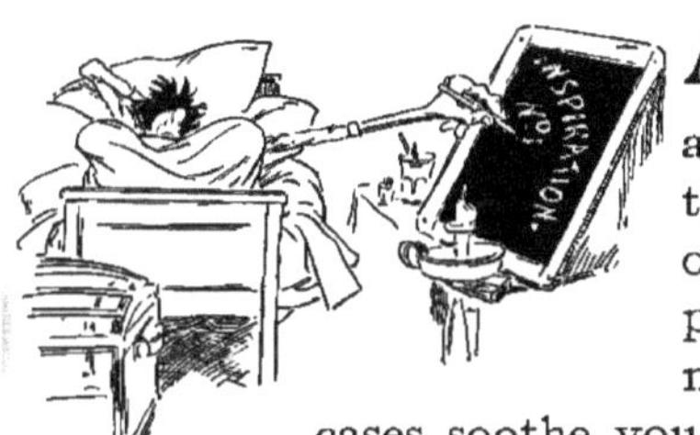

A SLATE or pad and pencil kept at your bedside (in a handy place), upon which to dot down inspirations that occur to you while insomnia prevails, will relieve your mind greatly, and in many cases soothe you back to sleep.

I don't know what inspirations look like, but I have often been awakened by them. After my kicking over more or less costly bric-a-brac in an effort to find a pencil and paper, my dear wife has assured the children that it was nothing more serious than an inspiration that ailed papa, and that without medical treatment or the aid of a doctor their father's condition would soon be normal—then he would see

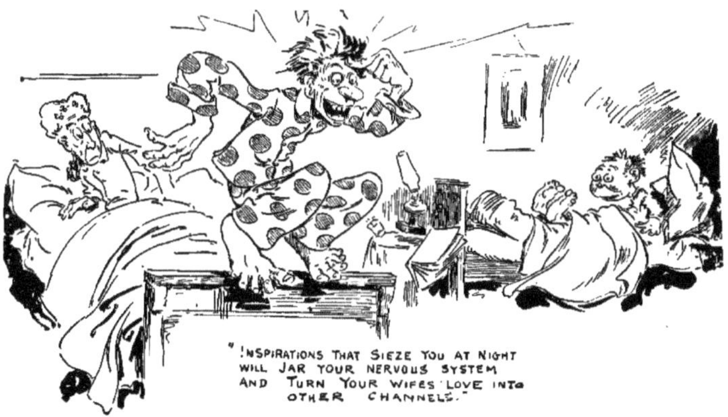
"INSPIRATIONS THAT SIEZE YOU AT NIGHT WILL JAR YOUR NERVOUS SYSTEM AND TURN YOUR WIFES LOVE INTO OTHER CHANNELS."

what a silly goose he was for letting an inspiration disturb him. Upon my word and honor, I'd rather be troubled by skeeters or fleas than inspirations, and so I have resolved to keep a slate and pencil at my bed-side.

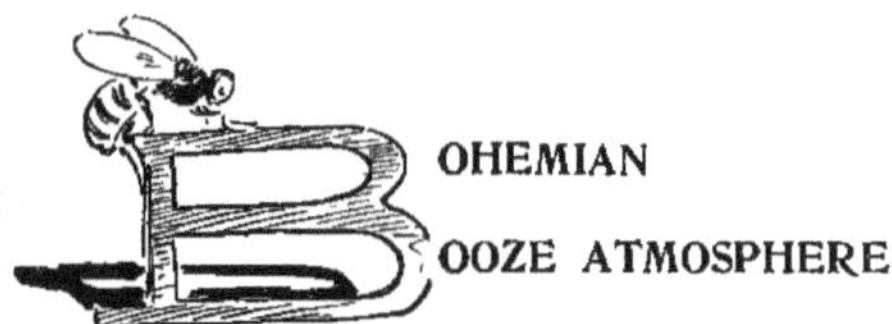

BOHEMIAN BOOZE ATMOSPHERE

MANY promising careers have come to an abrupt end through over-indulgence in "Bohemianism." A boy, when he enters the art arena, quite naturally thinks it the proper caper to become a thorough "Bohemian." To follow this life in its true sense is all very well; but the average art student is quite apt to mix it up too freely with beverages of amber and more ruddy tints—a nerve-wrecking and career-destroying course.

Bear in mind, strong beverages are no promoters of powerful ideas, nor is a torpid liver conducive to executing them. Being a head-worker you need rest. Get your natural rest, keep your liver in condition, so that you can enjoy your food; then you will also enjoy your work.

REVERSING A PHOTOGRAPH

In copying a side or three-quarter view photograph you frequently have occasion to turn the face in an opposite direction. To do this, just face the photograph toward a mirror and copy the reflection.

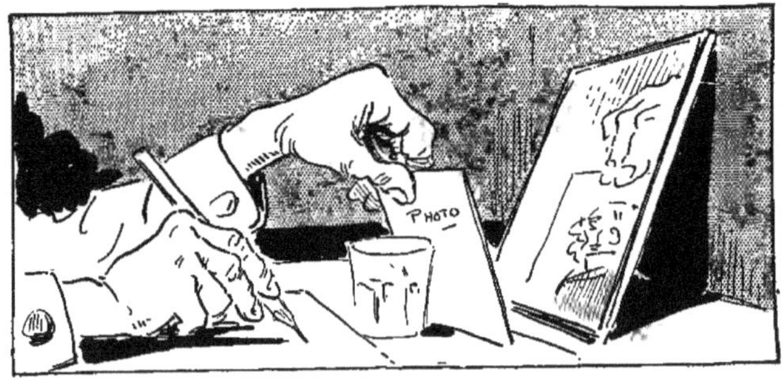

TO REVERSE A PHOTOGRAPH

The dotted work in the background of the above cut is what is known as the Ben Day process. It is largely used in lithography, in putting in delicate tints, and in many cases in filling in pen and ink drawings. A further description of this process would be of no particular value to the beginner. Your Art Director will explain this when necessary.

Writers, like doctors, often disagree. If you have already read the opinions of other caricaturists you might have noticed this fact. I am giving you advice from my point of view only.

A FEW WORDS ALONG STRAIGHT LINES

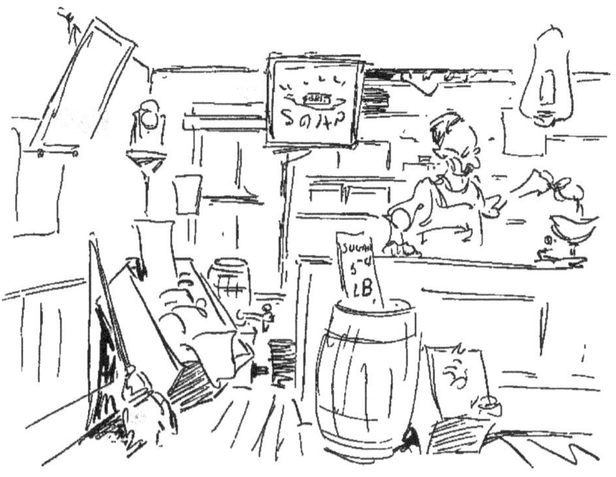

IN this sketch I have endeavored to show how the long straight lines should be disconnected by other objects cutting into them.

Observe the following rules when you are designing the background to a drawing. Avoid long straight or curved lines without some object breaking into them. They are inartistic and disturbing to the eye. The accompanying sketch illustrates how you can make your backgrounds interesting.

Draw in your background as though you were arranging a stage setting, putting the various pieces of furniture in such positions as to break up the monotony of blank space and long lines. Frequently a good play falls flat owing to poor arrangement of objects on the stage. I draw this comparison so that you will remember when at the theatre to note the stage arrangement.

The object in illustrating this matter is to impress it more vigorously upon your mind, for it is a well known fact that pictures speak louder than words; so I live in hope that should you forget my words you will not forget the pictures.

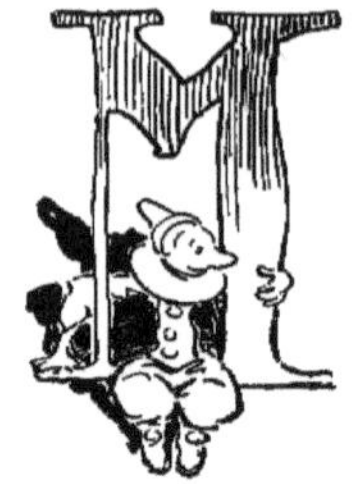

ANNER OF SUBMITTING JOKES IN THE ROUGH

WHEN you have established a reputation in the Art world, you need only send to the publisher a rough unfinished sketch explaining the joke. The editor, being familiar with the style and quality of your drawing, will advise you to proceed with it or inform you that it is not available, in which case you are out only the little time the sketch has cost you.

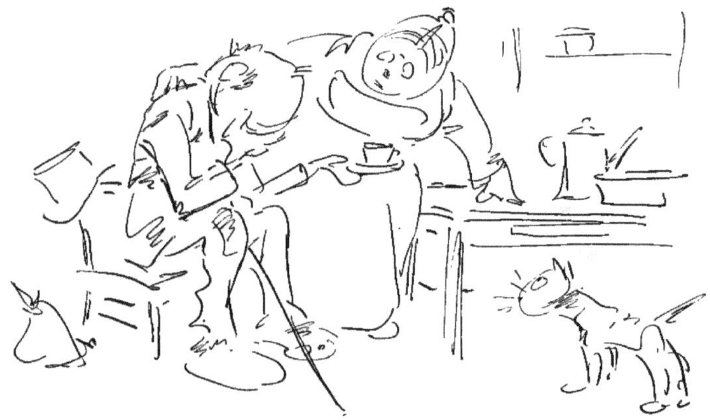

THE TIES THAT BIND THE RAILS TOGETHER

KIND LADY—Calm yourself, my good man; surely you must have some ties of affection in this world?

DISCOURAGED TRAMP—No; mum! I know no ties but dose what railroads is built on.

If you expect any recognition when you rap at the gates of paradise, for goodness' sake don't be stingy with your surplus knowledge; divide it with your struggling art friends.

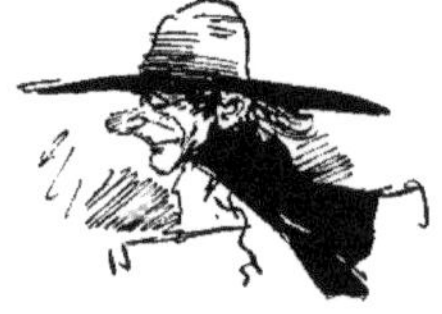

GESTURES

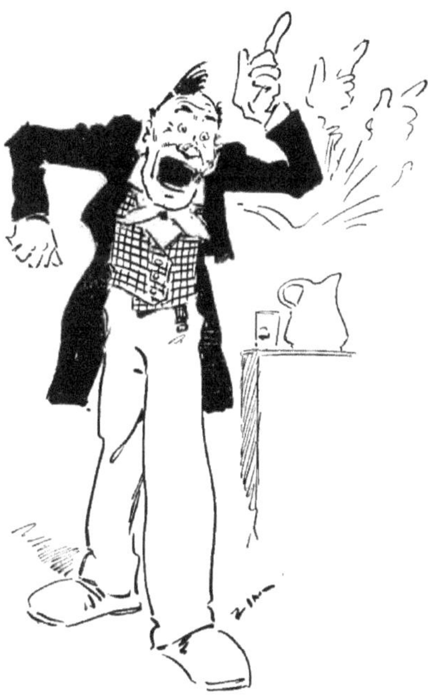

PERHAPS one-half of the people we meet "talk with their hands." The orator puts force into his remarks by using his hands to express his thoughts more pointedly. Many public men have peculiarities of gesticulation. This is a point worthy of note when caricaturing a public man.

DRAWING EXPRESSIVE HANDS

If you wish to put any particular force or expression into hands, use your own as a model. Your hands may contain too many lines or wrinkles; in that case draw only such lines as are absolutely necessary to make them natural, and full of bones and meat; your eye will guide you in observing the necessary from the unnecessary lines.

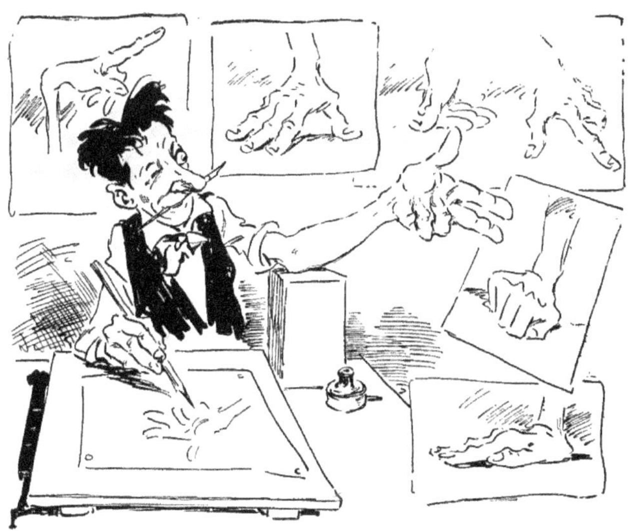

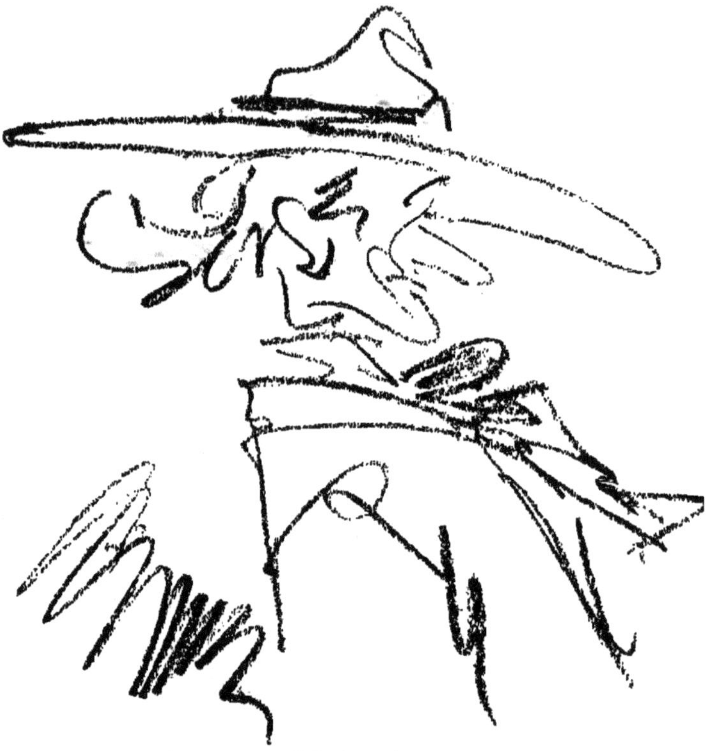

ROUGH PENCIL SKETCH OR LAY-OUT

SAFEST WAY TO SHIP DRAWINGS

NO matter how carefully you may wrap up drawings for shipment, they do not reach their destination in first-class condition. A tube containing drawings is liable to become crushed in transmission. Whenever I have anything of importance to put through the mail, to make it doubly sure that it will arrive free from mutilation, I saw off a section of one of the hind legs of the kitchen table and wrap my drawing around it. Where tables are scarce a broom handle will serve the same purpose.

Drawings wrapped in this manner will defy the ravages of the baggage smasher. Every day drawings are received at the newspaper offices in a horribly mutilated condition—the fault of the artist in every case.

The safest way to transmit drawings is by express with valuation attached. Then they are put through at the express company's risk.

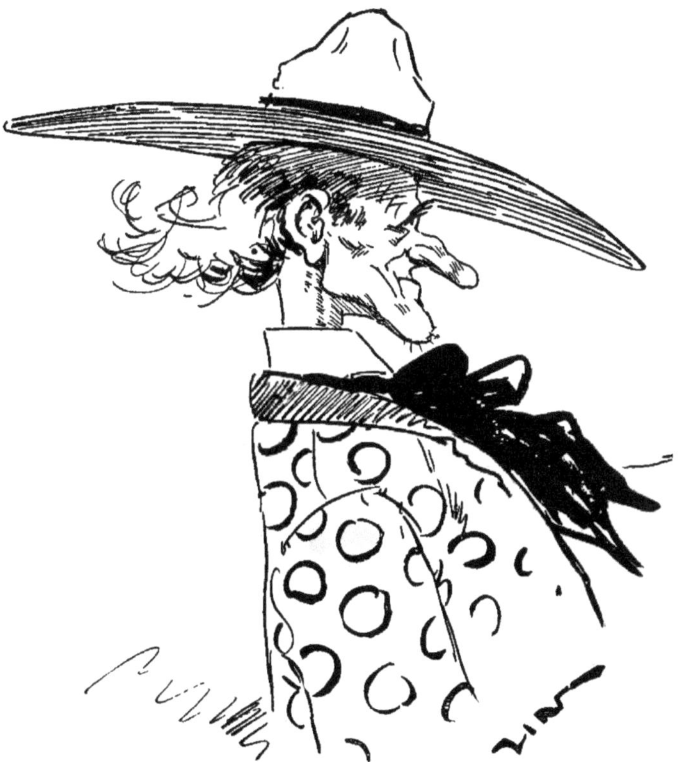

THE FINISHED PEN DRAWING, PENCIL LINES ERASED

THE COUNTRY POST-OFFICE

Did you ever take notice of the public bulletin board in a country postoffice? The postoffice is usually in one corner of the only grocery or general merchandise store of the settlement, and right next to the cod-fish and dried herring counter.

On the bulletin board, which is for the accommodation and enlightenment of the community, you'll find scraps of paper informing you that "Jonas Silleker lost his fals teeth las nite, and will pay a liberal reward for the return of same before Sunday mornin' at 10 o'clock, as he is invited out to dinner and must have 'em to fulfill the engagement. Price no object." And that Allen's mill will grind grist Monday. P. S. At too o'clock next week.

Lost articles are displayed on this board for identification, and to a man or boy who has a funny streak in his make-up, there is much food for thought.

Drawn on Ross' ruled Scratchboard No. 10. This board can be had in many designs. Send to art material stores for samples

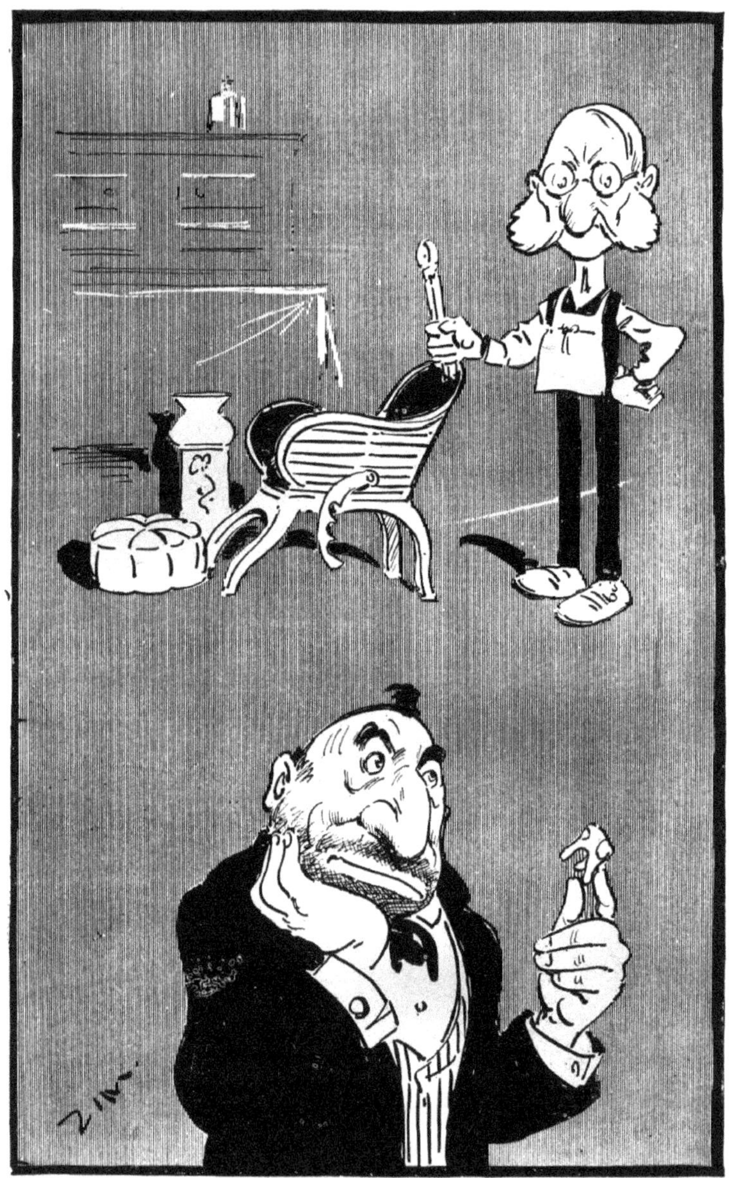

ECKSTEIN (after having tooth extracted): "I wonder eef he will allow me anydings for that 18 karat golt filling in dees toodh."

SPATTER EFFECTS

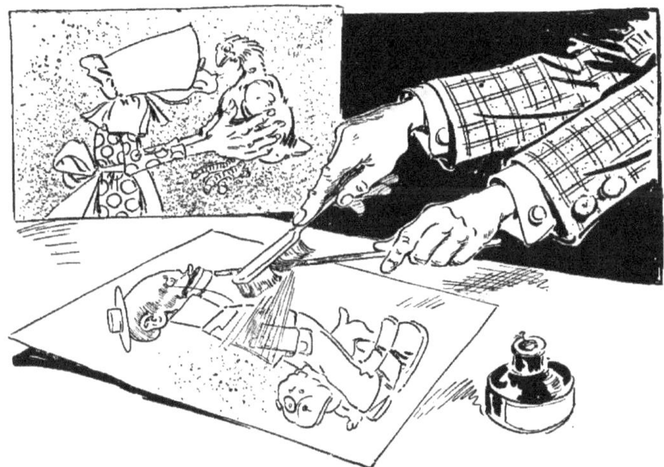

A VERY effective background may be made by introducing spatter work, the treatment of which I will describe, viz:

First outline your drawing with ink, allow it to dry, then cover with paper the parts you wish to protect, and leave the parts to be spattered exposed. Use a clean tooth brush. Swab a little ink into the bristles, then shove the brush across a stick or case knife.

SNOW STORM EFFECTS

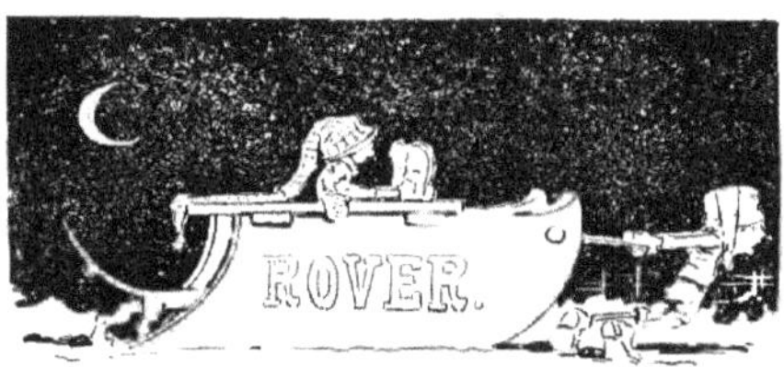

Snow storm effects may be had by spraying "white" (water color) paint upon the dark background in the same manner as above described.

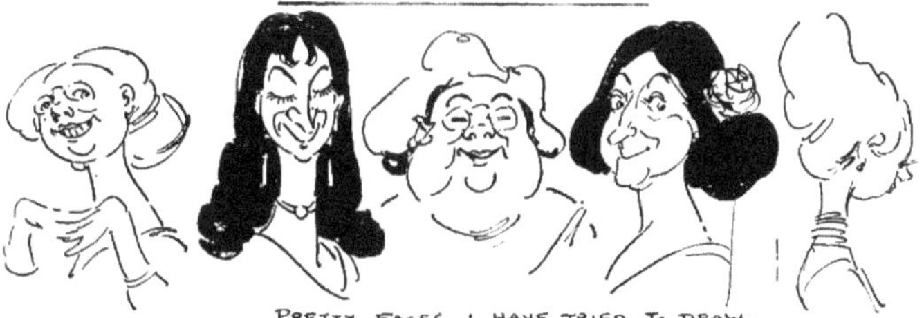

PRETTY FACES I HAVE TRIED TO DRAW.

SHOES THAT DENOTE CHARACTER

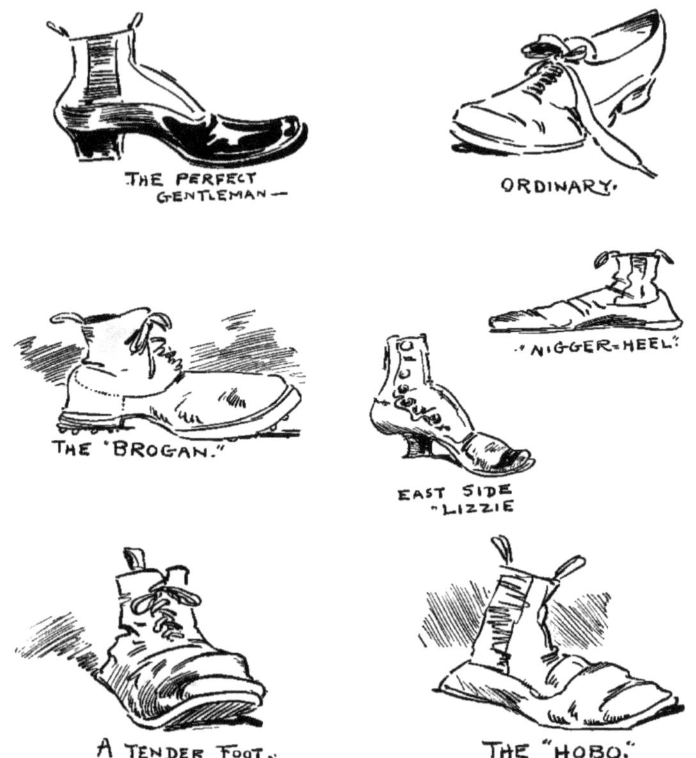

WHEN you make a character sketch be sure to append an appropriate foot.

The one great fault with the youth of to-day is that he reads of fabulous salaries paid to artists on newspapers, and without wishing to taste of the preliminary hardships which lead to large salaries, he expects to land right into a newspaper office: it's the proper treatment of details that earns big salaries.

JOT WHILE JOGGING

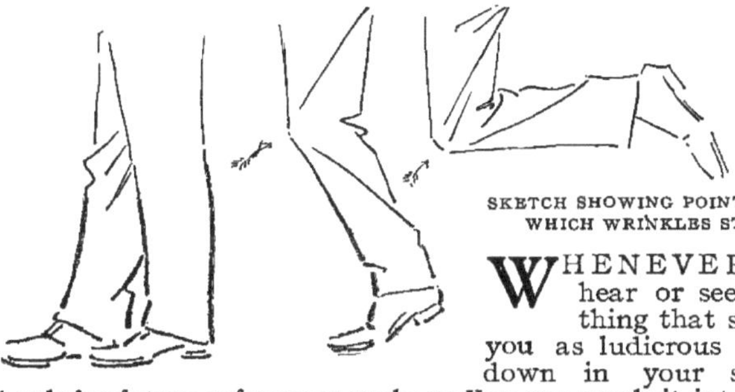

SKETCH SHOWING POINTS FROM WHICH WRINKLES START

WHENEVER you hear or see anything that strikes you as ludicrous jot it down in your sketch book for future reference; perhaps you can work it into cartoon some day. You have noticed the small boy on the street, no doubt, picking up scraps of string, pins, and rusty nails, and jamming them deep down into his pants' pockets. Did you ever stop to reason out what he intended to do with them? They were his stock in trade. When he had collected enough string he would wind it into a baseball. Heaven knows what he did with the rusty nails and pins! However, that is the way we, too, pick up material that others have dropped, and eventually weave it into a joke or picture.

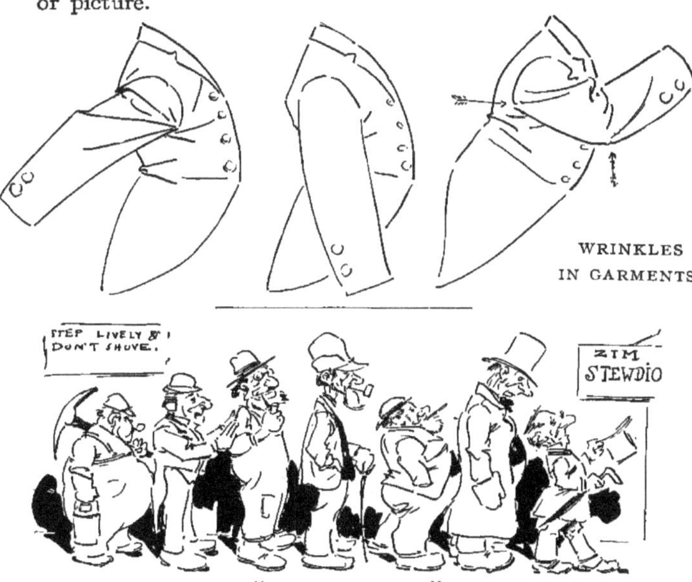

WRINKLES IN GARMENTS

"RECEPTION DAY"

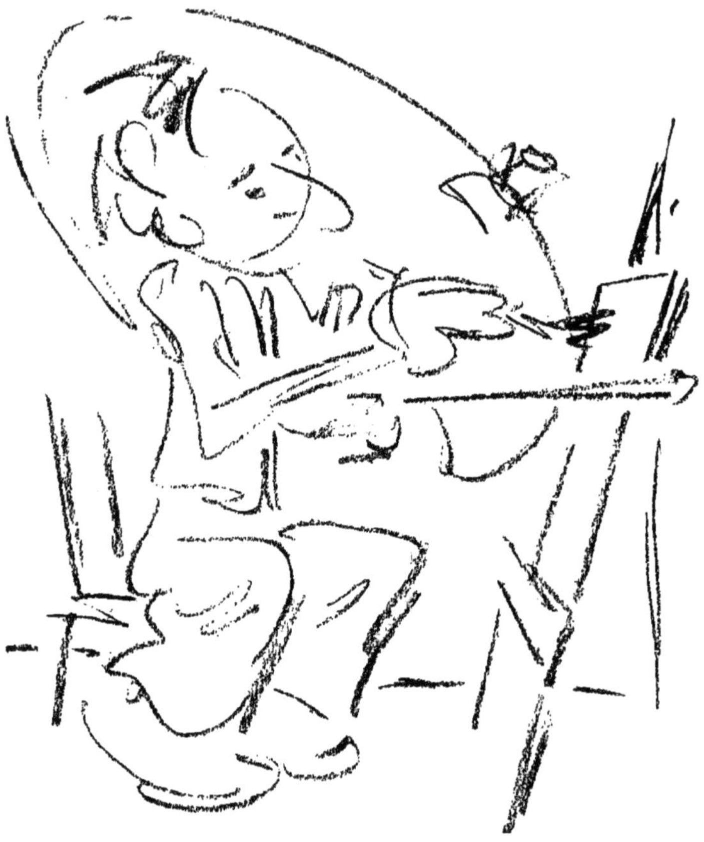

ROUGH PENCIL SKETCH

THE correspondence schools have made it possible for a boy to develop his natural gifts in almost any line of profession or trade.

Newspaper art, illustrating, cartooning and caricaturing seem to be playing a prominent part and at a nominal cost. Problems are worked out and trade secrets divulged which to the early youngster meant two or three years' apprenticeship without compensation.

If there is the slightest art germ lingering in a boy's sytsem the correspondence school will develop it.

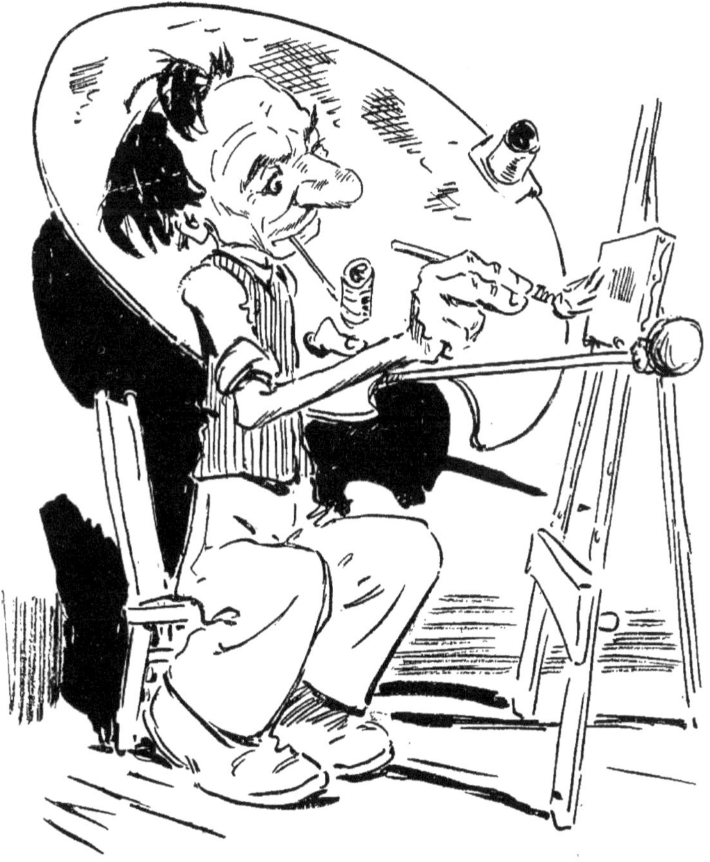

FINISHED PEN AND INK DRAWING

THE COST OF "LINE CUTS"

THE minimum price for line cuts is about fifty cents. That is, if you wish a single cut made one inch square it will cost just as much as a cut containing ten square inches. It involves the same trouble to produce the one as the other, but you can combine a lot of small drawings to be reduced on one large plate, then cut them apart, they will cost only the regular rate of five cents per square inch aside from the cost of sawing apart.

DRAWING FEATURES WITH THE AID OF A MIRROR

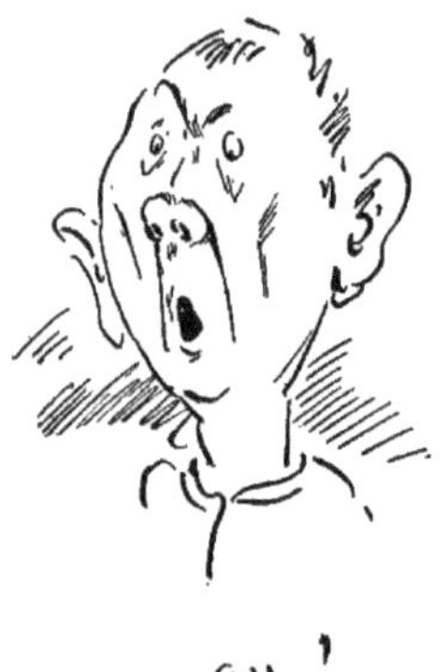

OH !

WHEN drawing distorted features you will observe that your own face assumes similar contortions. Like the tailor, when cutting a piece of cloth. He brings his jaws together in unison with every snip of his shears. You will find it much easier to depict an expression by using a small mirror, thus copying the necessary lines from your own countenance.

"OUCH !"

Beginners are apt to put superfluous lines into a face, and when the drawing is reduced these lines are brought closer together. The result is a botchy confusion of lines and the expression destroyed. Work up your faces with as few lines as possible, as the expression of the face has much to do with the success of a comic picture.

Just study these four sketches for a few moments; you will find them good examples of the effect produced by using a few lines only.

JOY

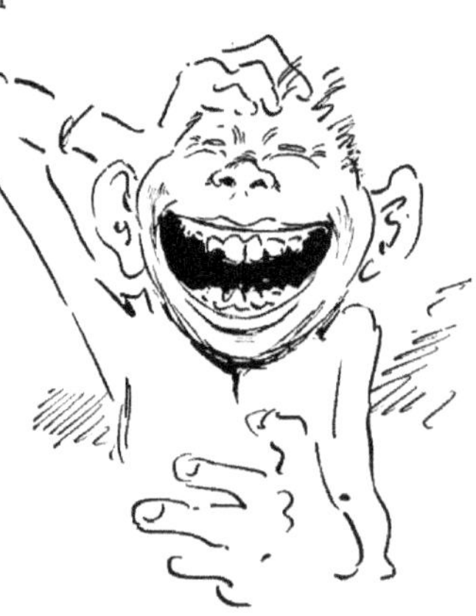

EXTREME JOY.

THE CARICATURIST: ACHES AND PAINS vs. HUMOR

THE caricaturist cannot always be funny. He has his aches and pains like other mortals. He sometimes bets on what he thinks is a sure thing and for a while has the humor knocked out of his "funny-bump." A bilious attack is not liable to yield side-splitting effusions; therefore, when you find that he is below his usual standard of funniness, you must make allowance for conditions which may have deprived him for the time of his drollery.

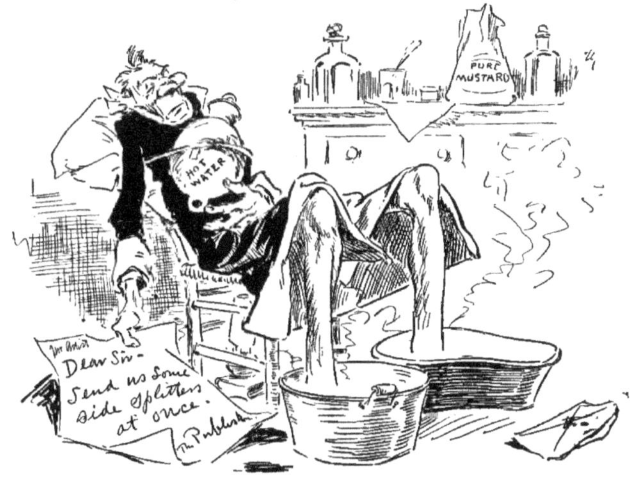

ONE ON ME!

I am not superstitious, but here is one on me. A friend, and a very successful business man, too, noticed that I was signing my name with a downward slant. Said my friend, "Never again sign your name downhill! Always sign it up hill, it looks more prosperous." From that moment I have signed my drawings up hill, and I really believe there was truth in his assertion.

HOW TO INVEST YOUR SURPLUS

As soon as you can afford it, especially if you have anyone dependent upon you, lay aside a part of your salary each week for life insurance. If you have no dependents, then take out an endowment policy for ten or twenty years, payable to yourself.

GOOD FROM CENTER TO EDGES

THIS book is like the pumpkin pie that mother used to make: Every bite is good and no particular place to start in.

There is no front or back to it—no special place where the villain enters and the green lights are turned on. Every page finishes its own chapter. The chapters come in small chunks and are easily digested.

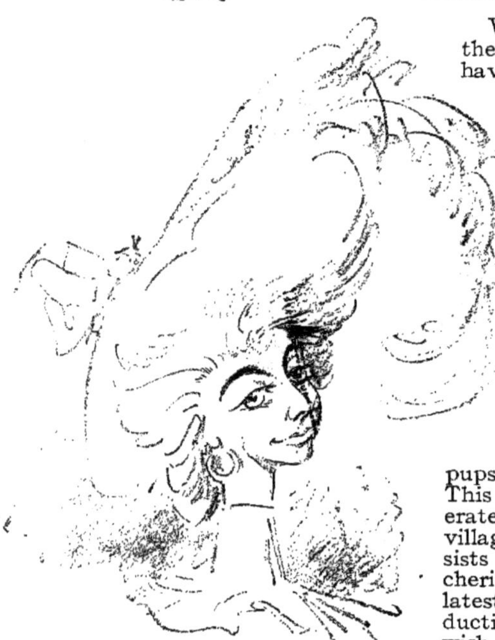

THE ABOVE SKETCH WAS MADE ON "ROSS" SCRATCH BOARD NO. 27, STIPPLE FINISH IN IMITATION OF LITHOGRAPH STONE

When you get into the public eye you have opened the way for innocent attacks upon your good name. For instance, many families in the middle and lower walks of life deem it an honor to name their last born after you. Others feel privileged in calling their pet pups by your name. This much you can tolerate, but when the village cigarmaker insists on placing your cherished name on his latest five cent production you begin to wish that destiny had been less kind to you.

This is what happened to me and it fell to my lot to make a label to fit the weed, a sample copy being first presented to me from which to draw my inspiration.

Let my own fate be a warning to fond mothers whose talented sons are forging to the front.

SINGLE OR DOUBLE

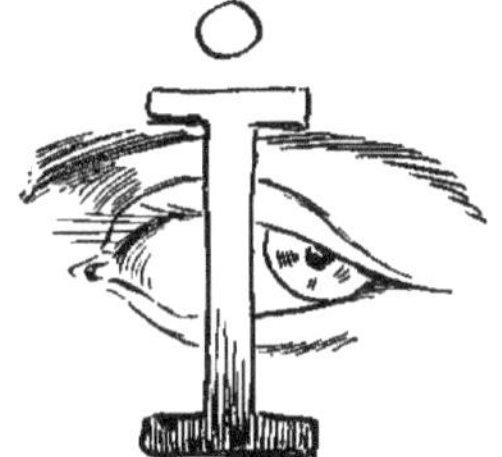

CANNOT say whether a man, in order to become famous as a caricaturist, should be married or unmarried. I have known both classes to succeed. In the face of the facts before me, it would be safe for me to state that a man, to be successful in any matter he undertakes, should be either married or unmarried.

BUSINESS LYING, IN WHICH ARTISTS ARE NO EXCEPTION TO THE RULE

Men are often obliged to lie in business. I have seen so much of this sort of thing that I can hardly refrain from doing so myself. I mean innocent lying, such as women are wont to do when the front door bell rings and the maid, under instructions, informs the ringer that the Mrs. —— has just left for Paris and would not return till fall. If you must lie at all, confine it to the six working days, and for heaven's sake hold the Sabbath sacred and untarnished.

VALUE OF EARLY EXPERIENCES

DON'T despise the hard knocks in early life; they will prove an after-benefit to you. You are gaining an education which will be invaluable in your profession. The different trades and callings with which circumstances have brought you in contact have taught you how various utensils are made, and how they are used, and how people feel and act who use them; and whenever you have occasion to make a picture embracing these utensils and people, your knowledge of them will save you considérable research.

I will enumerate a few of my most important shifts of profession before I reached the object of my ambition: Beginning with a baker's attendant, then office boy, newsboy, silk weaver, cotton spinner, farmer, fishmonger, wine bottler, sign painter and stencil cutter, besides a series of short term engagements too numerous to mention.

All this time, however, I had a desire to make a better man of myself, but owing to the enormous cost of engraving, there was little demand for artists upon newspapers.

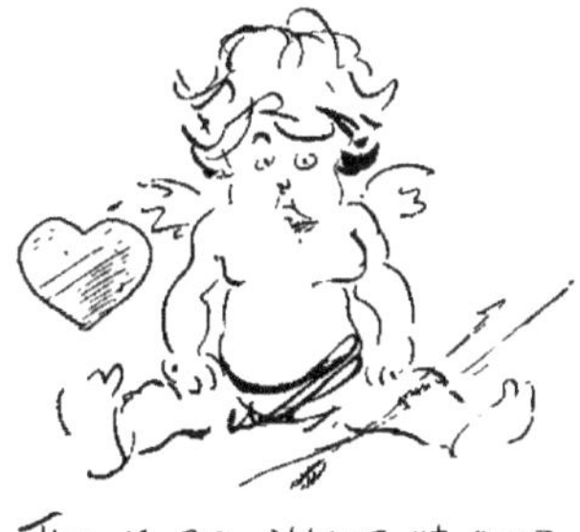

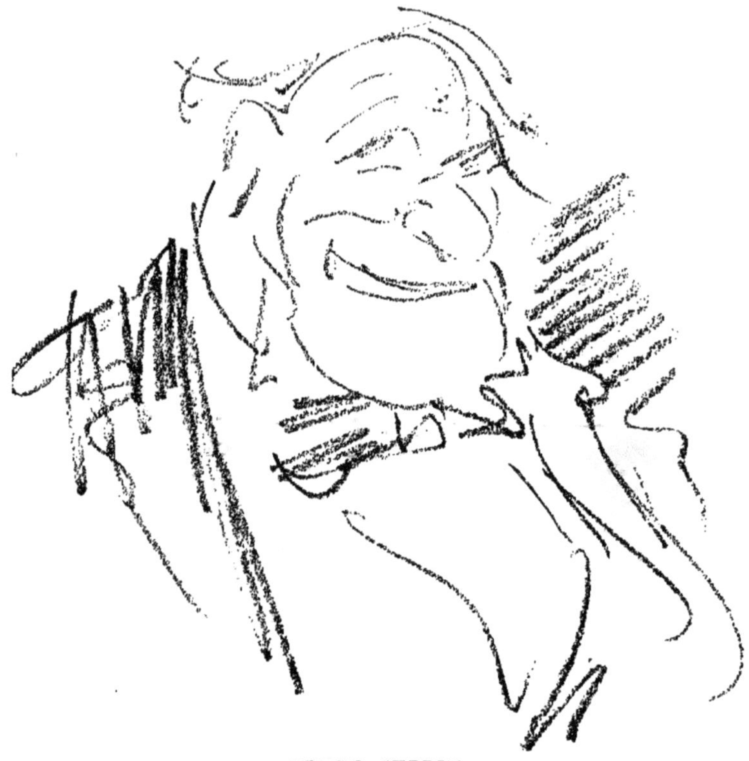

PENCIL SKETCH

STUDY THE COMIC JOURNALS

YOU'LL find it splendid practice to read over the jokes in the comic papers and build a picture to them in your own way. Do not offer such drawings for sale, as they are not original with you. Dispose only of such drawings as you are sure have never appeared in print.

SIGN PAINTING AS AN ADJUNCT

The sign painting trade seems to have played a prominent rôle in the lives of the men who have achieved fame in art and literature. There seems to be a sort of relationship between sign writing and comic art. There is no denying the fact that one, in order to be a good newspaper artist, should know something about lettering, for in many instances you will be called upon to make headings for stories and special column headlines. If you have ever had experience as a sign writer you will no doubt realize this fact.

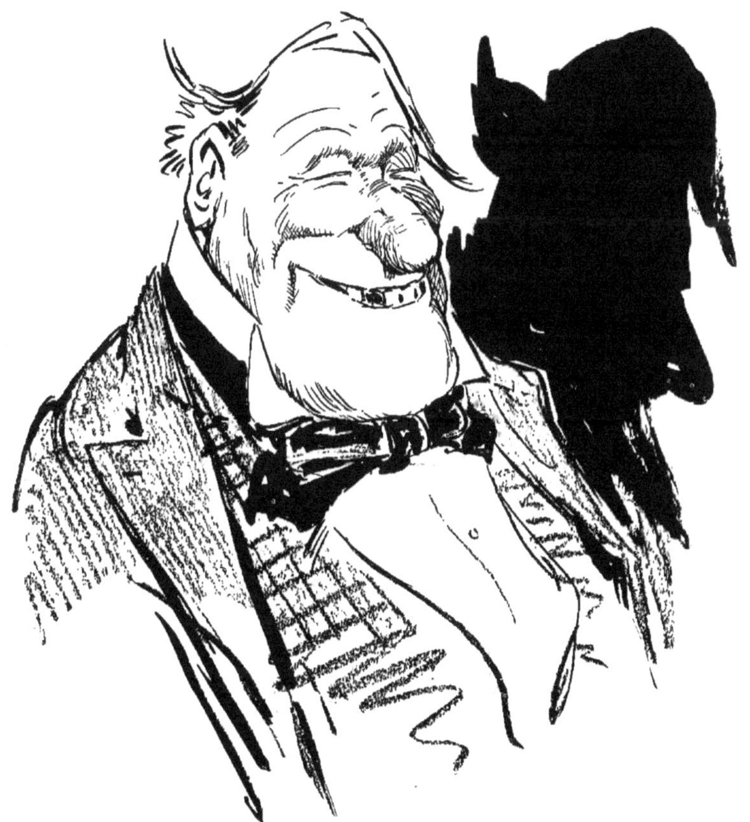

FINISHED DRAWING

THE Caricaturist should be considered in the light of a hero. He has the power to make men great who deserve greatness. Many political Shining Lights would have gone to the grave unobserved were it not for the pencil of the Caricaturist: and it is also well to remember that many who posed as "friends of the masses" have been sent into obscurity.

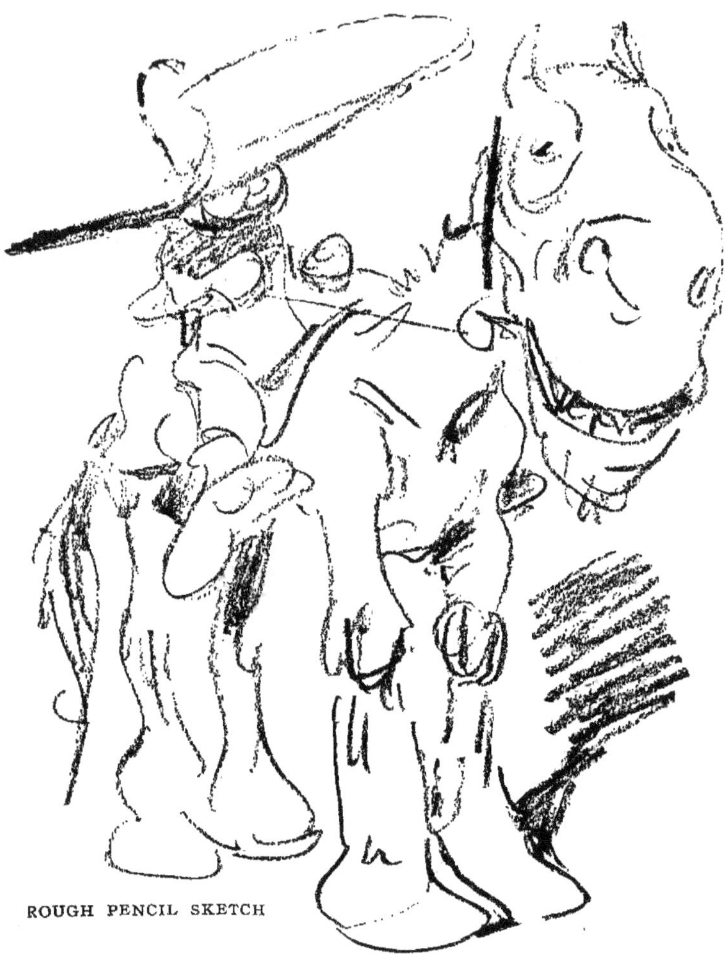

ROUGH PENCIL SKETCH

WELL, you never know what's in a name till the end is at hand and you count up your nickels. One prefers to be known to the world as P. Emerson Persimmons, another will sign himself briefly "Rip," or something equally appropriate or ridiculous. I notice, however, that artists run in classes according to the tone of their work. The drawing room artist invariably signs himself in fourteen syllables, while the comic artist is satisfied with one or two.

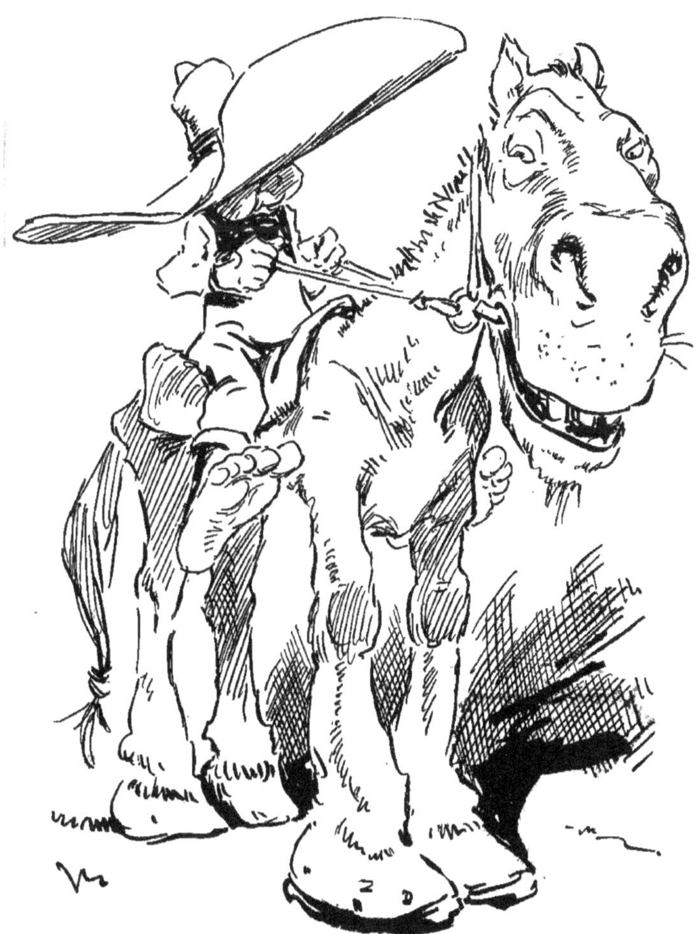

PEN DRAWING

HERE I show you (as in other cases in this book) a pen drawing as finished after a rough layout. (See page 46). How much the rough study and the finished sketch help you depends entirely upon how closely you go into the details in each drawing. Take the man's feet and watch the details: then examine in both drawings the hands and the head and you will thereby gain valuable experience.

THE ARTIST AND HIS IMPORTANCE

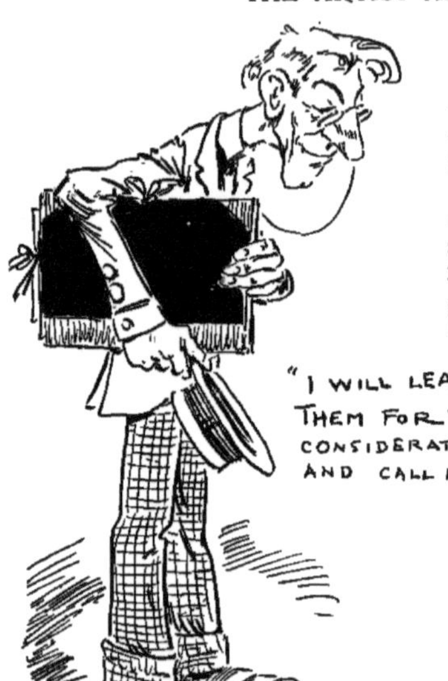

WHEN you seek the approval of publishers, don't try to convince the person to whom you submit your sketches that they are the best lot of drawings ever offered for publication.

Remember this person is an apt critic, hired for the purpose of selecting the most desirable work for publication. He may be the Art Editor. If so, his opinion is law in the Art Department.

If your drawings are rejected it does not signify that your work in not up to the standard. The Art Department may have sufficient material on hand for several issues. In that case, try other publishers.

Write your full name and address upon the back of every drawing and enclose stamps for their return.

THE ART EDITOR

An artist at any stage of his career approaching an art editor with a degree of modesty, will meet with due courtesy. Don't insist upon an immediate inspection of your drawings. An art editor is usually a busy sort of man, who jumps from one joke to another without rest. He looks upon original drawings as so much merchandise. Unless he has ample time to study the drawing and joke and the space it will occupy in the paper, he cannot give them the consideration necessary on short notice, and consequently they are turned down when a few days' delay might make them available.

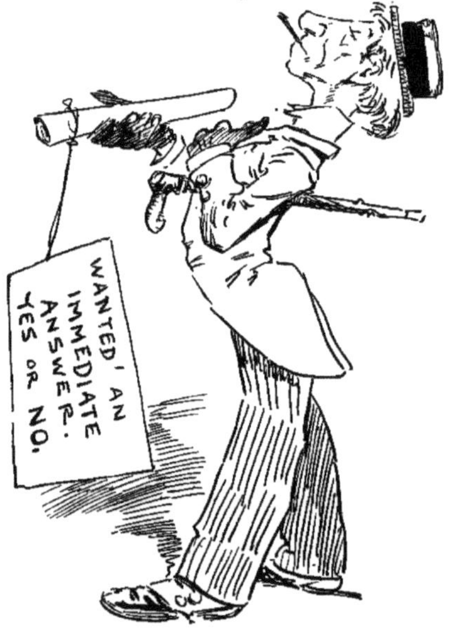

DRAWING UP AN IDEA

1. Write out your joke as briefly as possible.
2. Fix the picture in your mind, so that when you look at the blank bristol board you can already see your picture upon it (but in your mind).
3. Sketch the picture lightly and with some care upon the cardboard with lead pencil, then follow the pencil lines with India ink. When the ink is dry erase the pencil marks. If the sketch is to represent two figures, similar to cut on this page, begin with the two men in the fore ground and gradually work toward the background. Make your figures appear as though speaking the words of the joke—not with set jaws.

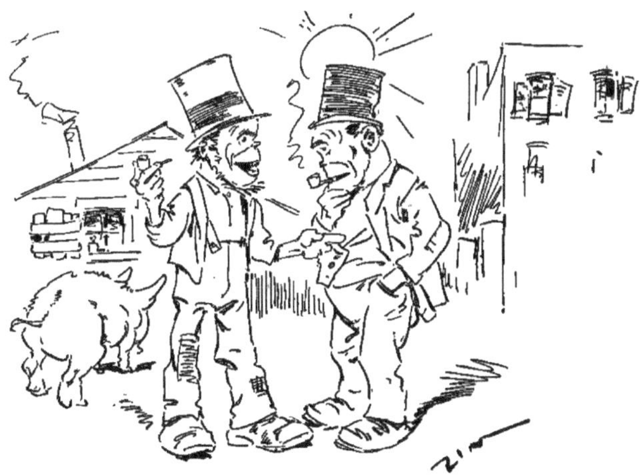

Black and white jokes are called "Comics" or "Insides," meaning for the inside of the paper. In making a "Comic" don't be too grotesque in your drawing—keep within the bounds of nature. There is an abundance of humor in nature without the slightest exaggeration; a little exaggeration flavors it, but too much makes it grotesque and hideous, instead of humorous.

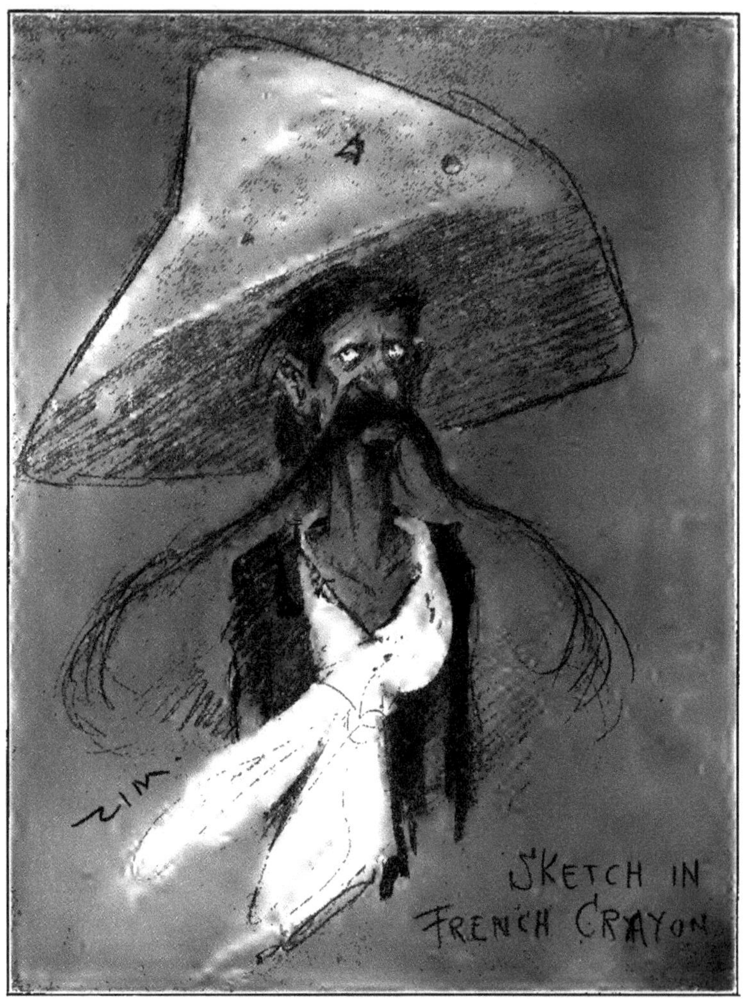

SKETCH MADE WITH FRENCH CRAYON UPON GRAY TINTED WATER COLOR OR CHARCOAL BOARD. SIZE OF ORIGINAL DRAWING, 15X20.

There is a preparation called "Fixatif," which, when you make charcoal, crayon, pastel or lead pencil drawings, you spray over the surface of your drawings with a blow pipe that comes with the outfit. This coating, when dry, will prevent the drawing becoming rubbed or marred.

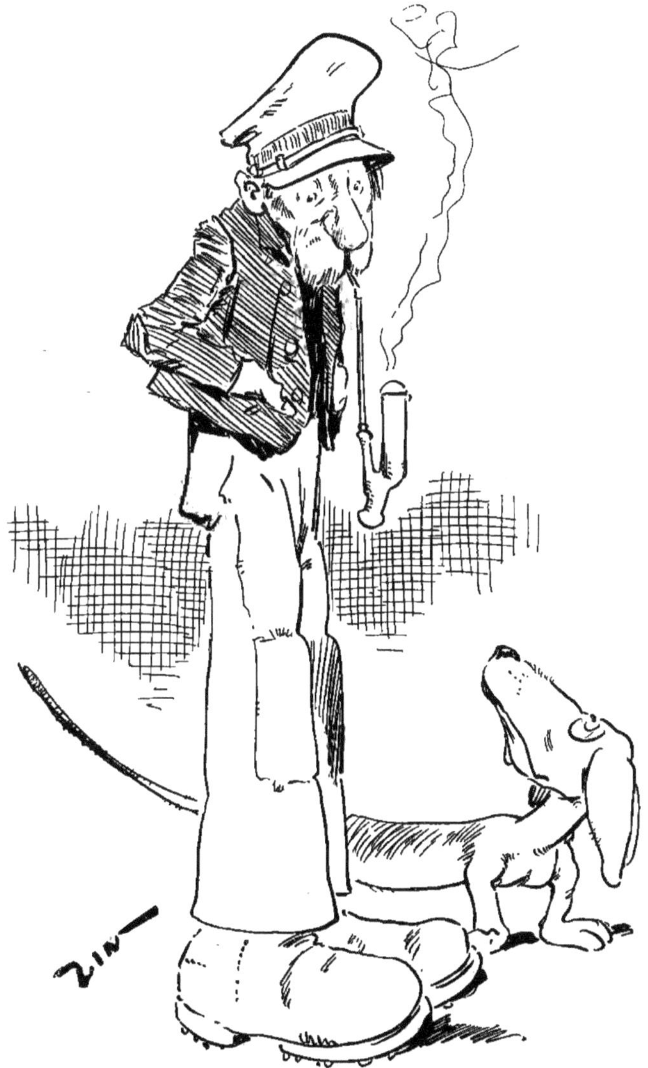

LINE CUT—CHARACTER SKETCH
Reduced to one-half the original size.

SUGGESTION OR IDEA SUBMITTED IN THE ROUGH

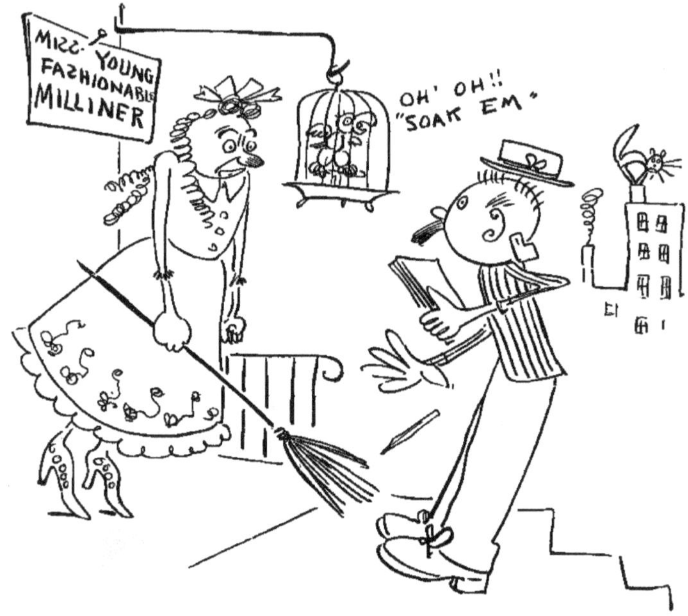

ALL THE DIFFERENCE IN THE WORD

CENSUS TAKER, to old maid: "How old are you, madam?"
OLD FAWN, reproachfully: "Sir!!! Such impertinence."
CENSUS TAKER: "Beg pardon, madam. I mean, how young are you?"

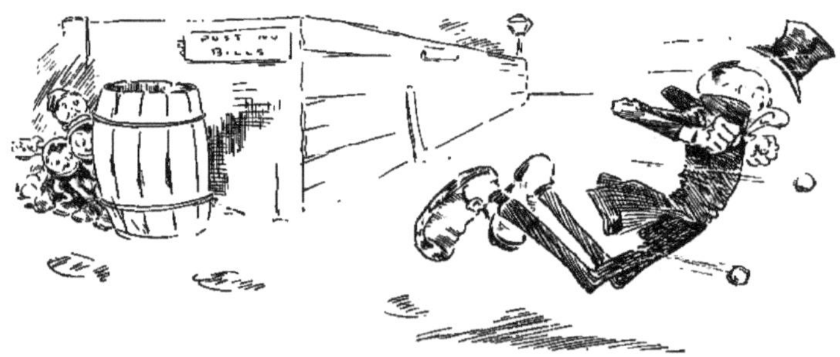

HIDES AND PELTS

A play on words, illustrating the sound of a word regardless of its real meaning.

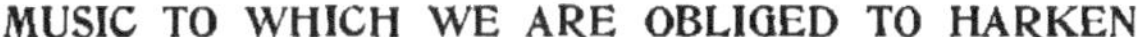

MUSIC TO WHICH WE ARE OBLIGED TO HARKEN

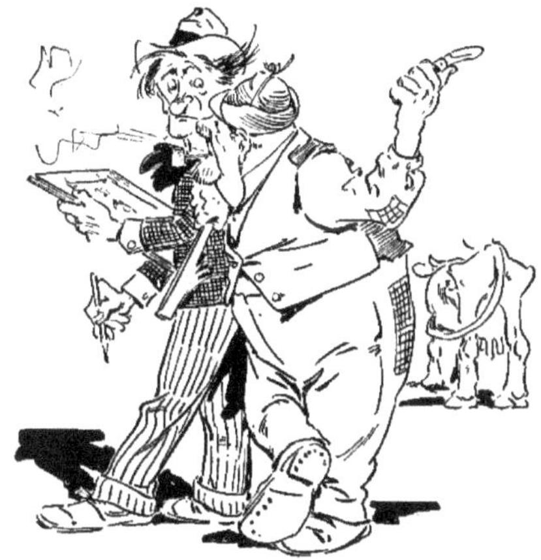

"THERE is a boy ten years old over in our town thet can drawer your pitcher so good thet you kin almost recognize it." Now what that boy wants to do is to learn to draw it so good that you *will* recognize it, not almost recognize it. There are a lot of almost artists in the world who can almost draw, and some of them are almost Gibsons, yet there is only one Gibson. The almost never looks any greater in the public eye than the ordinary run of men.

Gibson is a master. The fact is demonstrated by his army of imitators, and the reason of it is: he is strictly original.

PLUG HAT AND UMBRELLA

Perhaps the hardest simple object to draw correctly from memory is a silk plug hat; it is so perfectly shaped that the slightest discrepancy in drawing it is perceptible.

An open umbrella is also very difficult to draw correctly without a real one as a model. Give a little of your attention to the plug hat and the umbrella.

Sometimes a drawing can be made very effective by putting in heavy black shadows, as I have shown in most of the drawings in this book.

In caricature there is a happy medium between the grotesque and the sublime; when you reach that point in your drawings, stop.

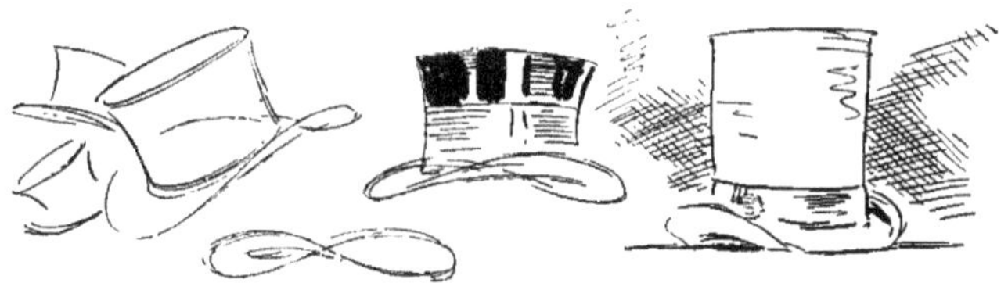

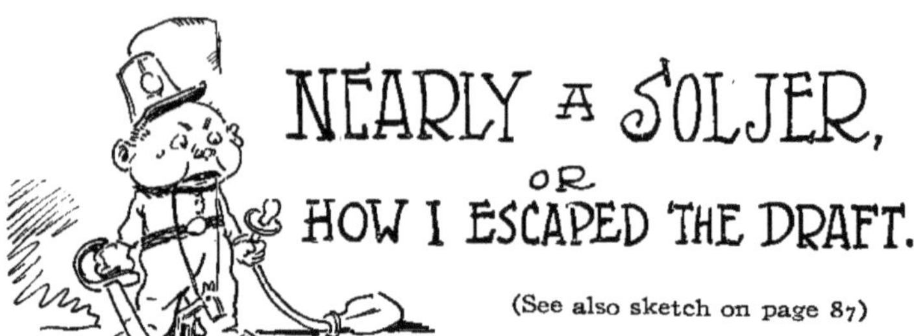

(See also sketch on page 87)

WELL do I remember the struggling days of '61. I was born the year following. Nevertheless, I had fight in me the moment I crossed the threshold of my father's and mother's home and made myself welcome. It was in Basil, Switzerland, where most of the Switzer cheese is made, and I suppose my Franco-German blood was sizzling and asserting itself.

I remember distinctly the first news at the happy hour of my birth was of the conflict on American soil. I longed to go at once. My parent could not bring me as he had his day's baking yet in the oven. As young as I was I could readily understand the situation and I brooded constantly over the fact that the conflict would be at an end ere I could reach the divided United States. I became a "Perfect Brooder."

Alas, such is the luck of those who are not born early in life. My good parent, to pacify me, promised to arrange a special war in France for my benefit, which he proceeded at once to do. First taking me to an uncle's home in Alsace, so that I might study the political conditions and military situation of that country. Seven years later, after getting the Franco-Prussian war well under way, I bundled up a few doughnuts and sailed for America, where all was quiet and peaceful again.

Since that period my life has been pretty well thrashed out by biographers, but never have they touched upon this very early and most important data.

Truth, every word of it,
I assure you.

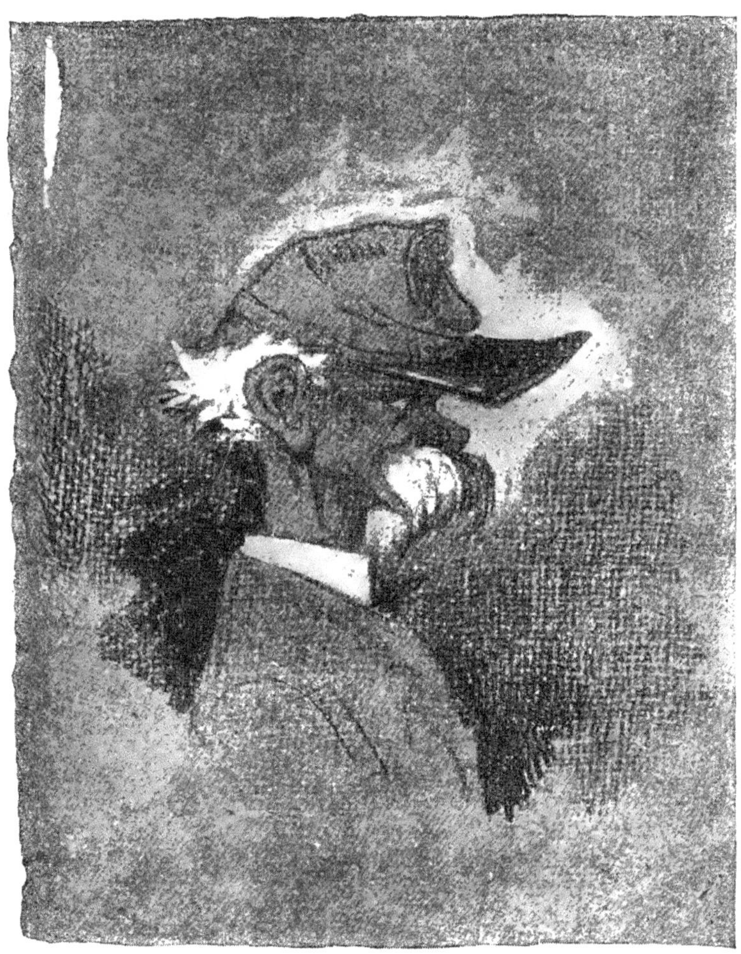

COMMON PACKING BOARD. SIZE OF ORIGINAL, 10X13

Crayon drawing made upon common gray packing cardboard.

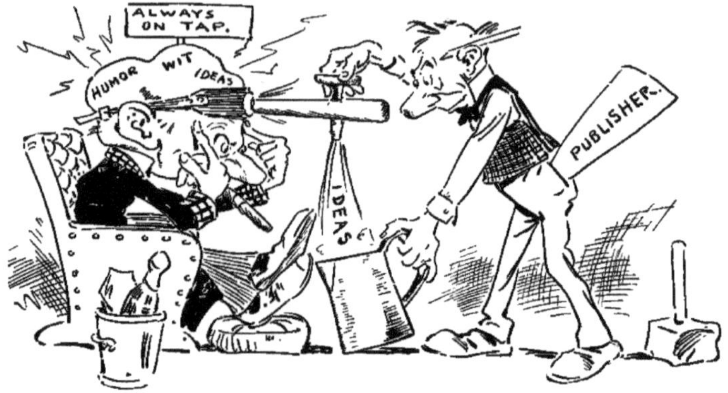

THE PROLIFIC MAN

WHENEVER you hear a man declare himself so prolific in ideas that he could fill a comic paper every twenty-four hours with his outbursts of side-splitting humor, you may depend upon it that there is something radically wrong about the person. The man is yet unborn who is so profuse in acceptable ideas that he could do the work of four or five or ten men. He might create lots of ideas that may seem the essence of wit to himself, but not to millions of people for whose amusement they are intended. The public is the best judge of a good joke. A paper catering to the tastes of the general public must have as much variety as possible, both in drawing and ideas. Publishers recognize this fact, and for that reason no one single artist is ever allowed to fill the entire paper.

In newspaper art there are three distinct branches: political cartooning, comic art and society drawing. The artist who can picture a drawing-room scene to perfection will be less forcible in comic work, it is like comparing the ring-master with the clown. Both of these functionaries know all about the circus, but neither could fill the other one's place. You should decide which branch of the art you like best, and try to make a success of the one you are most fitted for.

SOLILOQUIZING

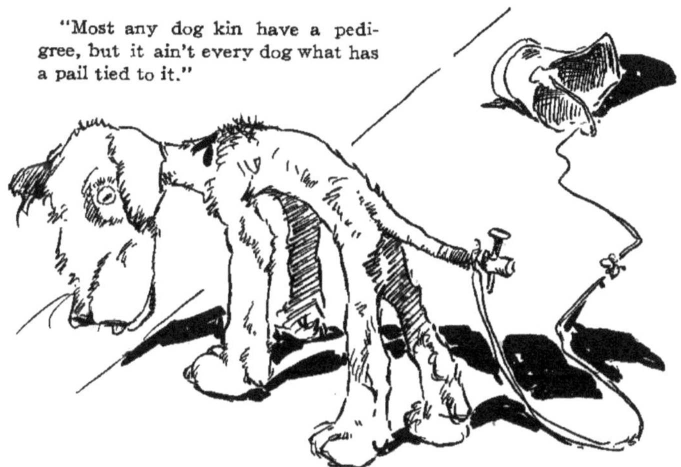

This style of joke is called a soliloquy, which means talking to one's self.

COLOR VALUES IN BLACK AND WHITES

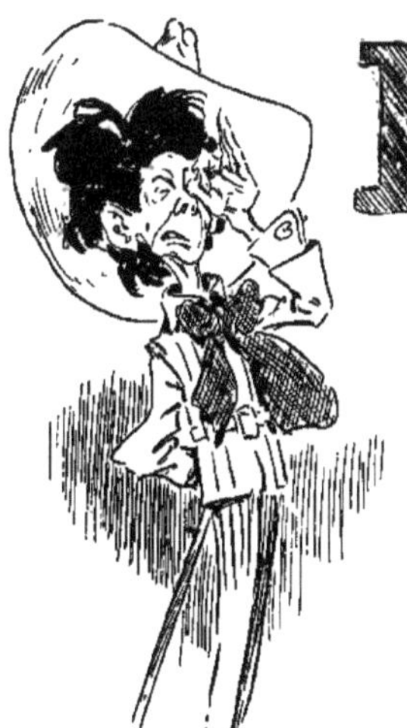

IF you are not familiar with pen and ink drawings and do not understand color values (lights and shadows), you might draw as nearly as possible in outline and gradually develop into the former. One is apt to overdo his sketches u n l e s s he knows exactly where and how to put in shadows to get the best possible results.

DON'T BE TOO NERVY

SHOULD you at some future time be commissioned to sketch faces at a convention, in a hotel lobby, or in the street, don't be too nervy. Don't plant yourself before the individual and stare him out of countenance—the person might be sensitive. You will make him feel unpleasant and perhaps cause him to change his expression, so that you will be unable to get a good likeness. If you are too bashful to ask consent to sketch him, don't display your nerve

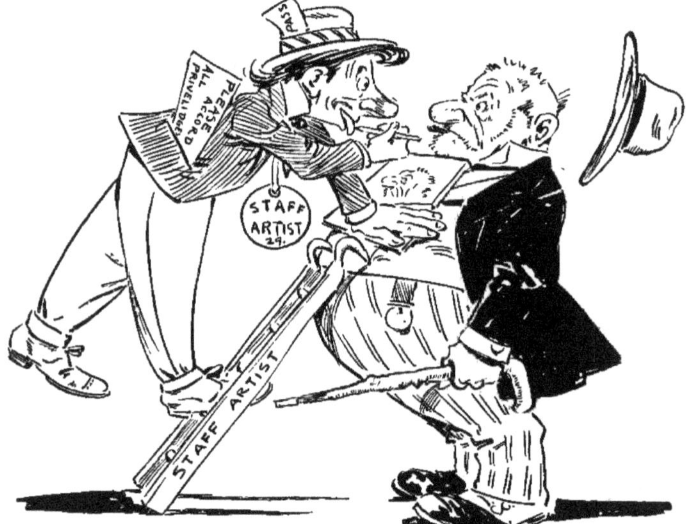

by staring him into submission. It is not at all difficult to perform your task of sketching your subject—it can be done in a sly manner entirely unbeknown to the party being sketched. When your caricature is published the individual will be dumbfounded to see himself in print.

Many times, while performing like duties, I would under the pretext of sketching some other object cast side-glances at my subject, keeping him unaware of the fact that I was caricaturing him. I felt satisfied at gaining my point and having made no one unhappy or uncomfortable.

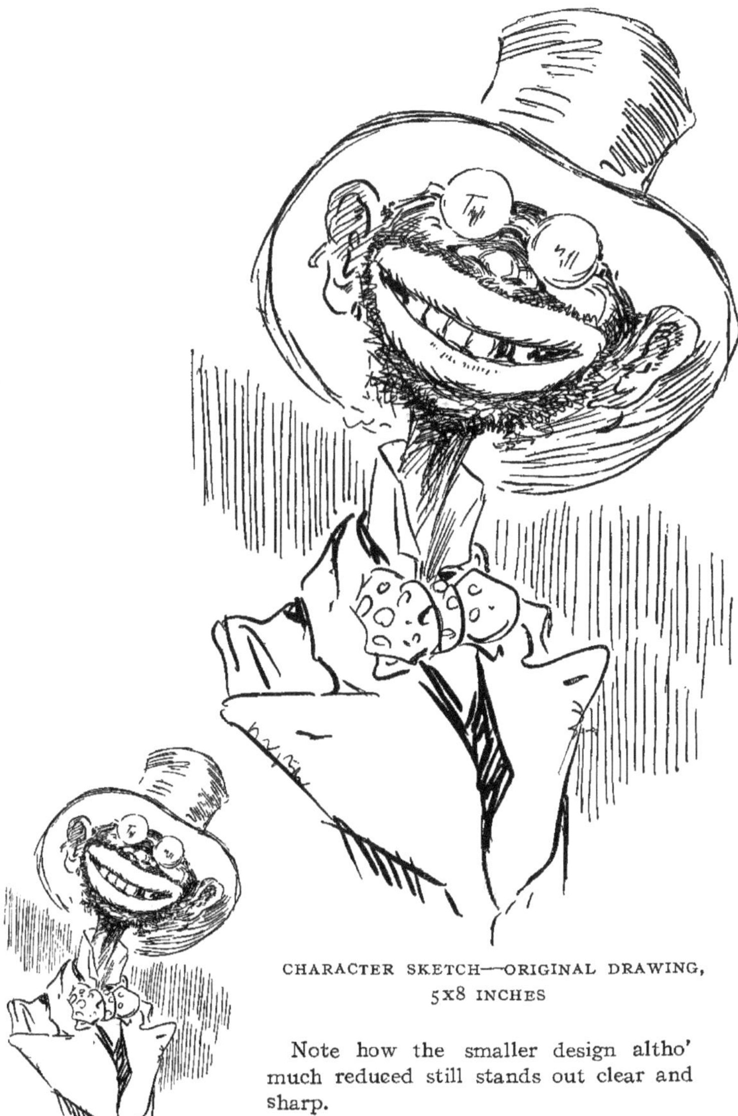

CHARACTER SKETCH—ORIGINAL DRAWING, 5x8 INCHES

Note how the smaller design altho' much reduced still stands out clear and sharp.

COMPANION PICTURES

TWO or more companion pictures telling a story are called serials, or in speaking of them in another sense, one would refer to them as a series of drawings. The story usually starts off in a normal state and ends in acrobatic confusion. For instance:

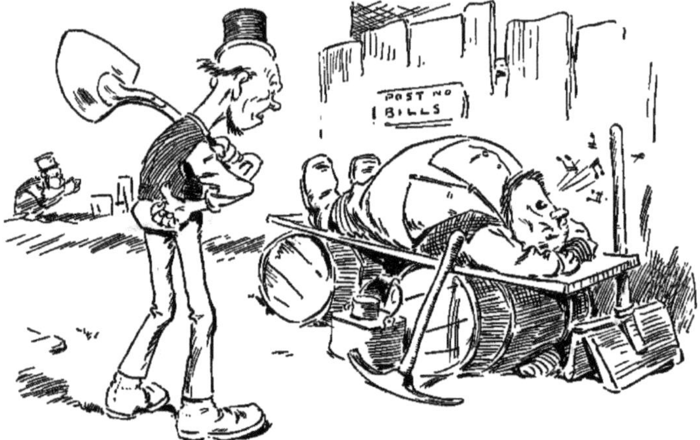

"There lays poor Finnegan, dead to the world, and divil a bit does he know phat a good toime he's havin'!"

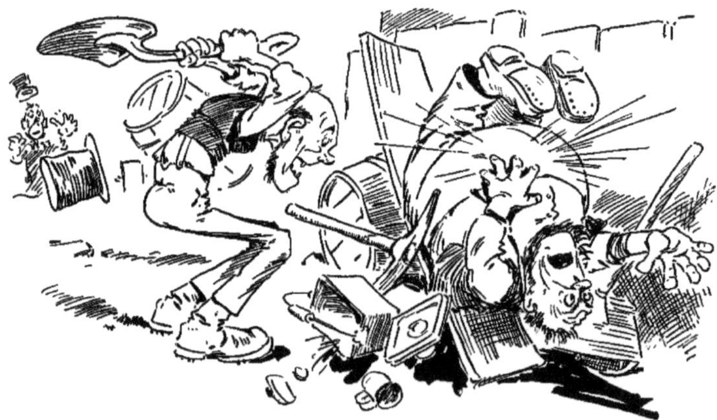

"Oi say, Finnegan, wake oop! and see how yer enjoying yer schlape."

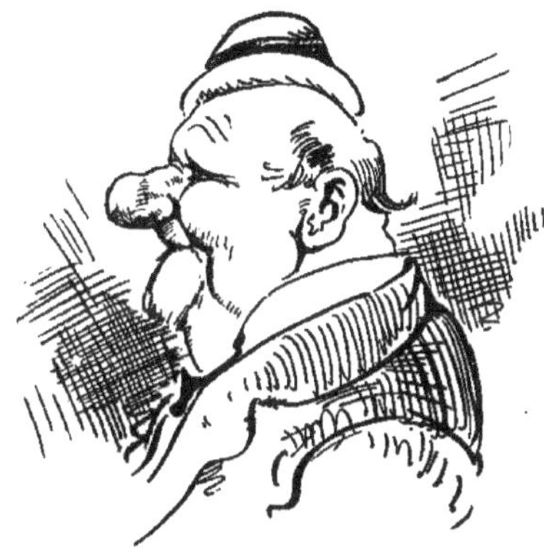
THE SAUSAGE FACE

DON'T WASTE YOUR GENIUS

REFRAIN from caricaturing acquaintances, unless you are sure they are not of a sensitive nature, else you may incur their enmity. If they are sensitive or vain they do not deserve the attention of your pencil or pen. You may ridicule, but don't offend.

I was sixteen years old before I earned anything more than board and clothing, then I secured a position with a pictorial advertising sign concern, and I received nine dollars per week the first year and fifteen the third. Then an opening presented itself, and I gave up my fifteen dollar job for a five dollars per week salary on a New York illustrated paper. I knew, however, that with my love for comic art, energy and perseverance, all of which I had a plenty, my salary could not remain long at such low tide. I soon got acquainted with advertising publishers who offered me commercial work. After a while I had quite a clientelle outside of the office, so that hardly a week passed that I did not have $50 or $75 in my pockets above my weekly salary from newspaper work. So I say, don't expect to become a full-fledged high salaried artist in twenty minutes. Sooner or later an opportunity will loom up, then grab it, even at the sacrifice of another job.

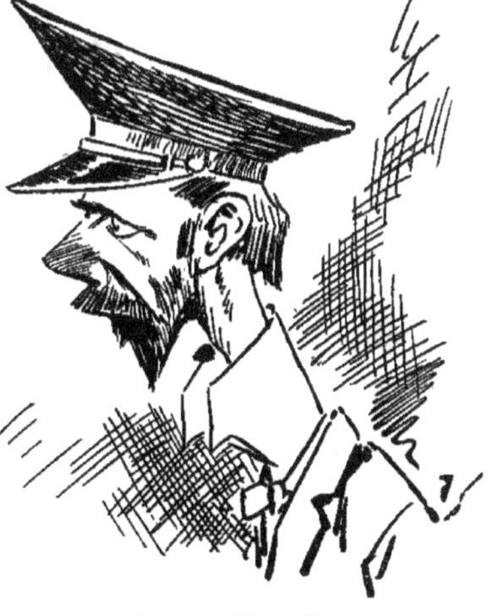
THE AUTO FACE

GOOD PRACTICE

I DON'T wish you to confine yourself entirely to my methods — you should read the opinions of others as well. We do not all work alike, consequently we cannot think alike.

Give, for instance, ten comic artists the same joke to illustrate, and you will see that not two of them will grasp the situation alike.

It would be good practice for the beginner to take a published caption from one of the comic papers (ignore the picture entirely) and work out the situation in his own way, just for practice.

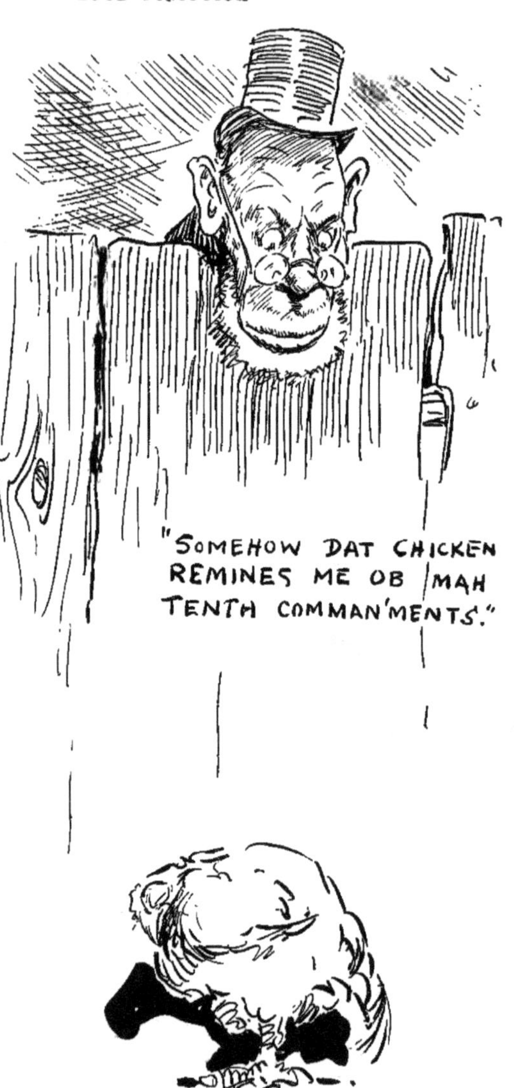

PROPER BALANCE

BALANCE your figures properly. Don't make them appear as if they seem about to tip over; if you find it difficult to do so, then draw up and down lines upon your cardboard (as indicated by dotted lines) where the figures are to stand. These lines will guide you in keeping the figures plumb.

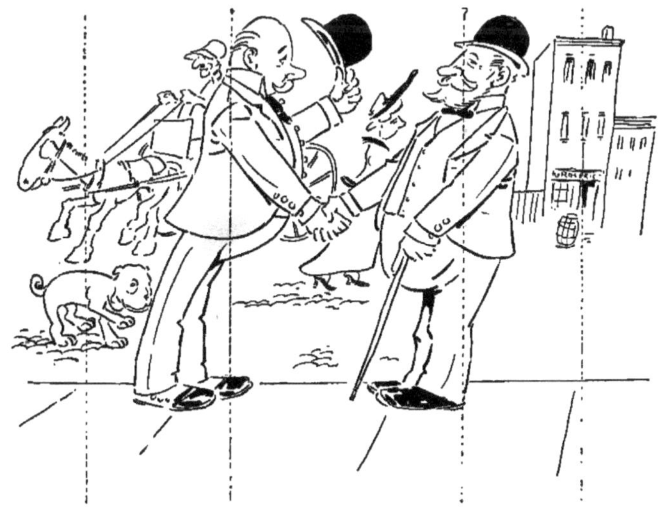

REDUCTION OF DRAWINGS

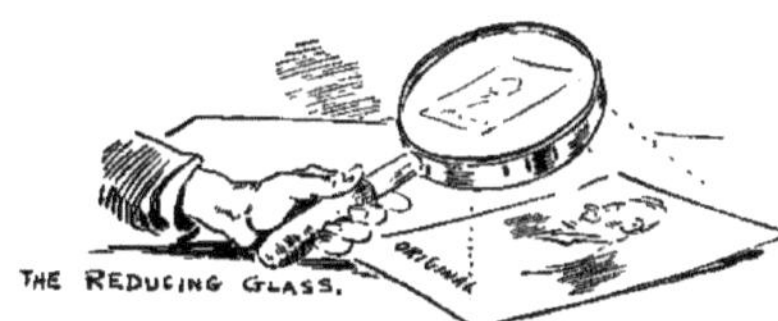

THE REDUCING GLASS.

It is wise sometimes to sacrifice good drawing for effects. I mean by this, that a drawing made large and carefully treated may not show up so well when reduced as a drawing treated with more vigor and dash. A bold, dashy drawing will stand a greater reduction with better effect. By using a reducing glass you will be able to determine the amount of reduction your drawings will stand. A reducing glass is the opposite to a magnifying glass. The former has both sides of its glass concave. while the latter is convex. They can be procured at artists' or opticians' supply stores.

RELIEVED BY THE LAYING ON OF HANDS

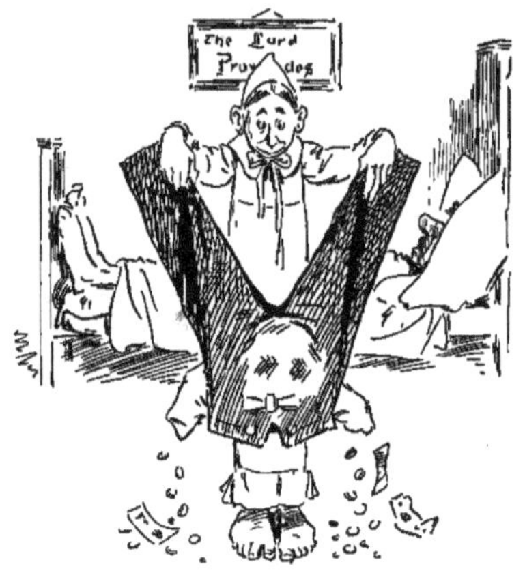

DRAWINGS based upon puns or parodies on popular songs and slang phrases, although ever so well applied, become tiresome. Don't harp on this class of joke, only turn out one occasionally. The ordinary dialogue is the most marketable. Always place your figures in a position in keeping with the wording of the joke. The reading matter to a joke is called the "caption." In speaking of it use this term, as it covers all that applies to that part of the pictures.

SUPERSTITIOUS

Portly Parker: Hello, Brown! You are getting thinner and thinner every day. That's a bad, bad sign.

Skinny Brown: Say, old man, do you really believe in signs?

Portly Parker: Of course I do; and always did.

Skinny Brown: Then if you can turn around without discommoding yourself just read the one behind you.

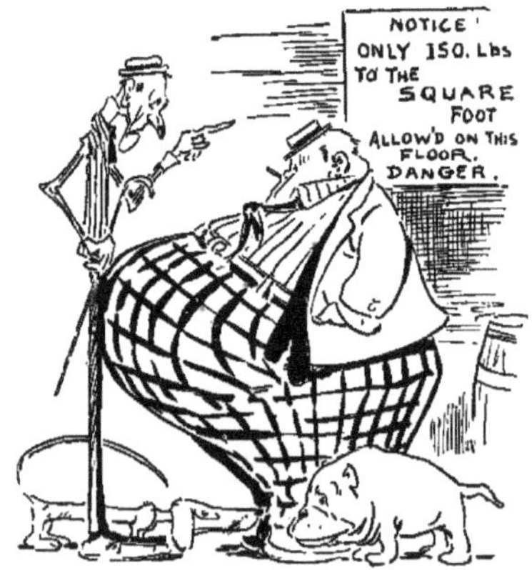

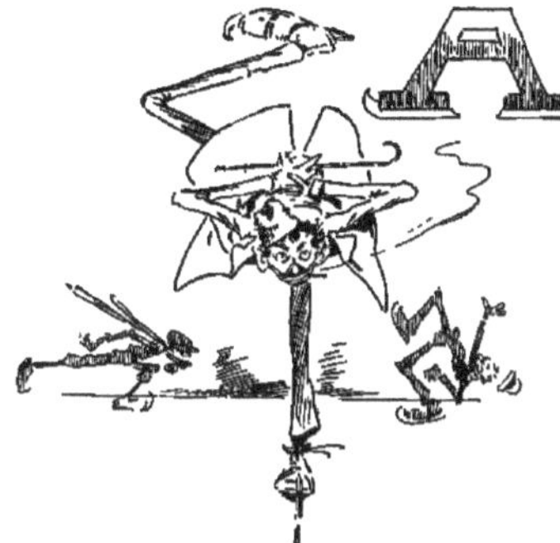

ACROBATIC DRAWING

Acrobatic poses, or figures in evolution, require a stretch of imagination. It would be next to impossible to find a man who in the name of comic art would be willing to receive a hook to the solar-plexus from a playful mule, so you must draw entirely upon your imagination for all such attitudes.

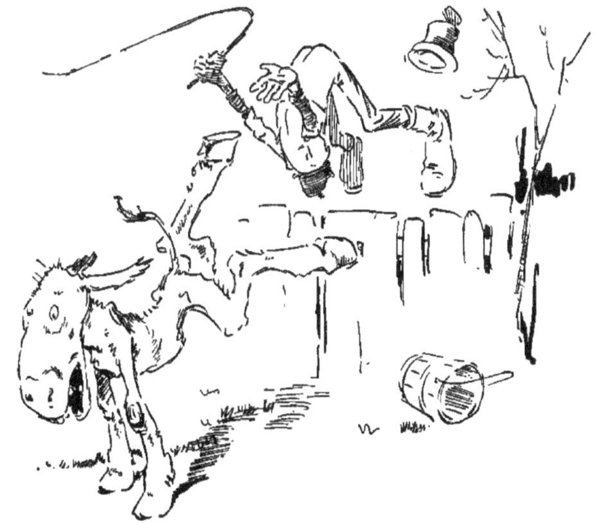

THE COMMERCIAL SIDE

You may possess a fair knowledge of caricature without my advice or guidance, but there are many things pertaining to the commercial end of the profession which all students should take into account. To make a drawing is one thing; to dispose of it quite another.

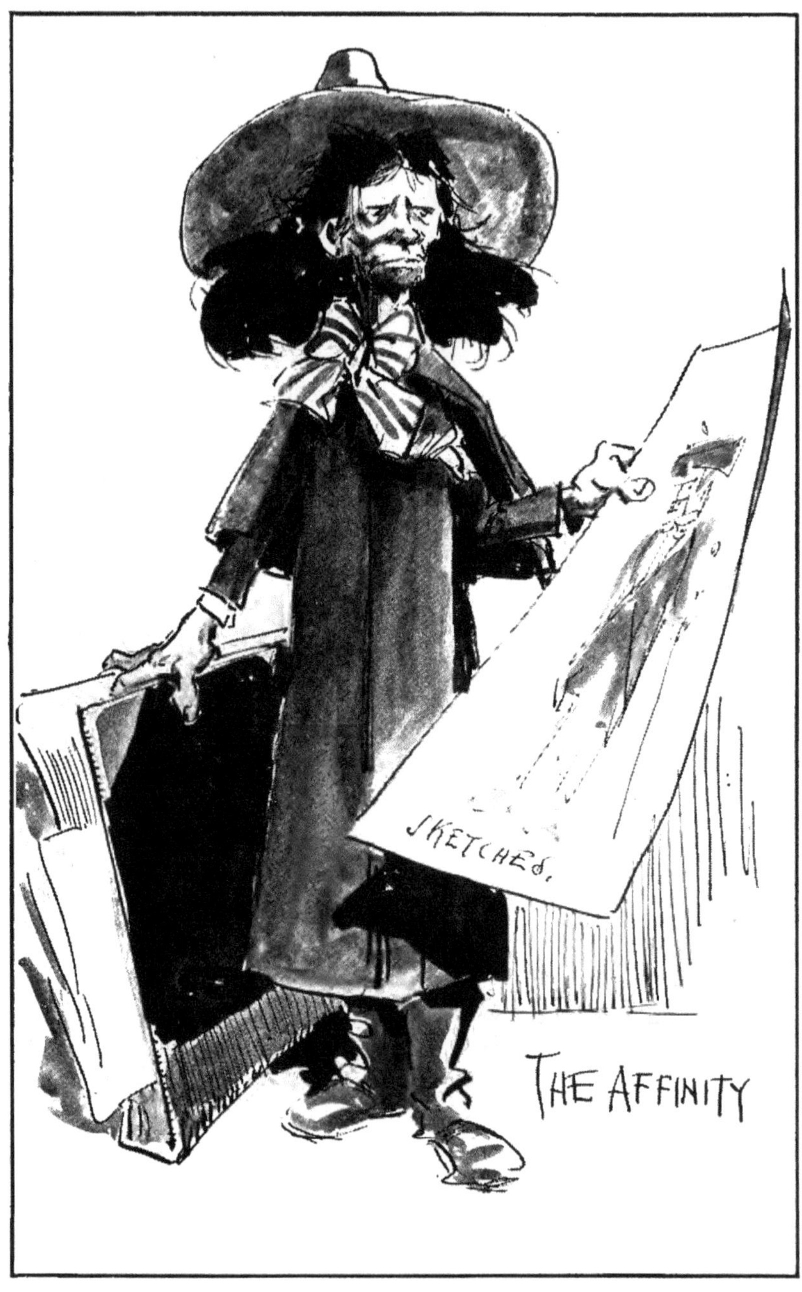

"I have noticed with extreme sorrow the utter lack of real art and merit in your alleged humorous publication and having your interests deeply at heart, I pray you to consider this symphony in sepia. I shall be most happy to permit the publication of this precious work in your periodical. My price is one hundred per drawing. I shall call for my check in the morning."

This sort of artist gets fifteen per instead of one hundred for his recious symphony in sepia.

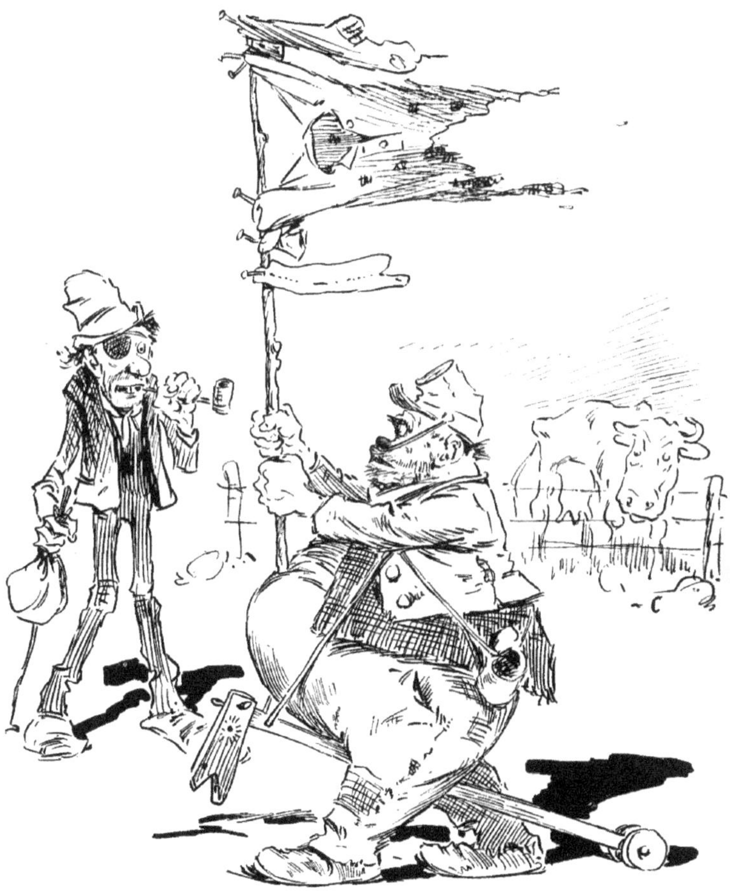

TWO EVENTS IN ONE

Blinky Bliss: "What's dem! battle flags?"

Rocky Ruggles: "Naw! Laundry. It's me good luck to have de anniversary of de fall of Wicksburg come on my annual wash-day; so I'm dryin' me linen an' celebratin' de joyous occasion at the same time."

THE HOBO BRAND

THE Tramp or "Hobo" affords much material for fun. He can be made humorous and genteel, or dirty and disgusting. It is advisable to make him not too genteel nor too disgustingly dirty.

HOBO: "Well, I swan! if me valey haint fergot to fill me matchsafe agin."

TWO IMPORTANT DONT'S

Don't insist upon sending your drawings to a busy artist for his inspection and criticism. Remember it involves considerable work, which he is expected to perform without pecuniary reward. The simple inspection of your work is not all that is expected of him. There is, besides, his criticism in writing, which in itself is more annoying than his other daily labors. Then there is the repacking, addressing and remailing of your drawings. This robs him of valuable time. In many instances postage is even omitted, which is a serious oversight, and shows a lack of appreciation of the favors you anticipate. Don't forget to enclose stamped and addressed envelope, whenever you desire a reply.

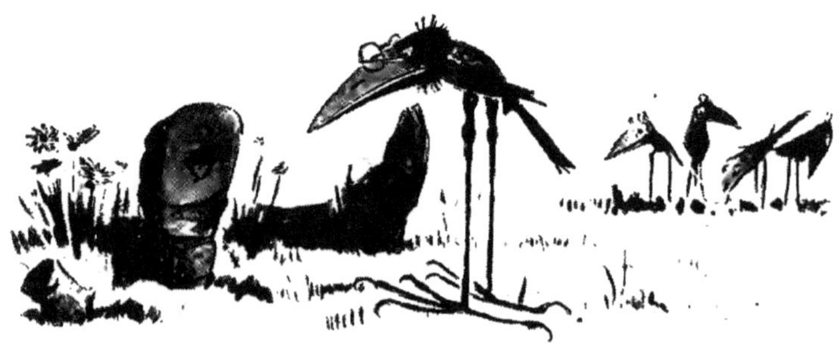

THE CORONER'S JURY

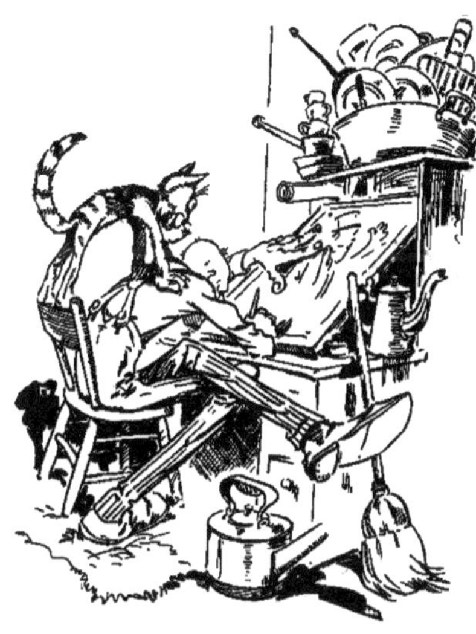

A MAN'S OWN CASTLE

A MAN'S own castle is the proper place for his art workshop, for then the whole family can enjoy his genius. He feels perfectly at ease. Things look so different, so domesticated, as it were, and so unlike the dull life of the studio.

I intended no reflection upon the management of my household when I made this picture, as my wife always asks of me before doing so if I object to having the dishpan left upon my desk while she sweeps down and dusts the cobwebs in the kitchen. Well, as I would not for the world have the dishwater soiled with dust and cobwebs, I assure her in gentle tones that she may bring in the stove and sink also. I want her to feel perfectly at home in her own house above all things.

Never place a valuation on your drawings, the art editor will attend to that and send you a check for the sum *he* considers them worth to his publication. You little know the public's wants—the success of an artists' efforts depends upon the way they are read by the public. Often a feeble joke meets with great applause; while many a powerful joke (in the judgment of the artist) has fallen upon the public like an icicle.

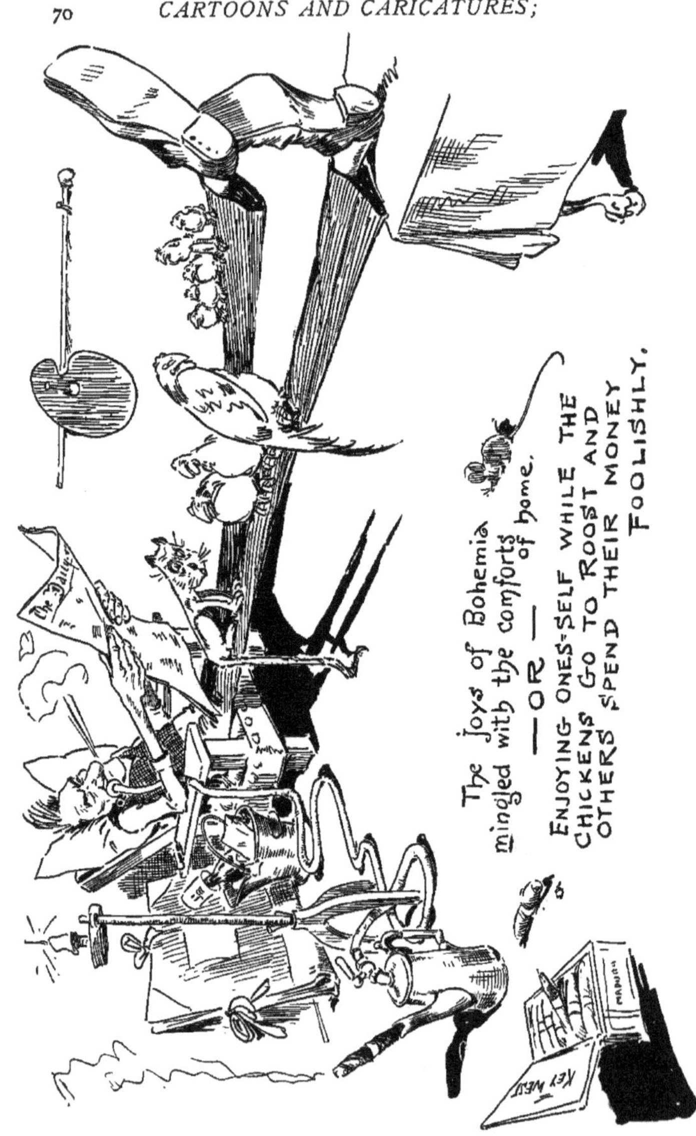
The Daily
KEY WEST
The joys of Bohemia mingled with the comforts of home.
— OR —
ENJOYING ONES-SELF WHILE THE CHICKENS GO TO ROOST AND OTHERS SPEND THEIR MONEY FOOLISHLY.

A FEW "POINTERS"

A JOKE, whether told by word or picture, should be brief. A sketchy background lends a sort of reckless abandon to the picture, which is pleasant to the eye.

Drawings should be made at least twice the size they are to appear in print. This gives you a better opportunity to work up the detail; the word "detail" meaning any accessories that have no direct bearing on the joke itself, but which add bits of interest to the picture.

You should not be harsh in your caricature of women. It is neither cute nor gentlemanly to injure woman's vanity by caricaturing her.

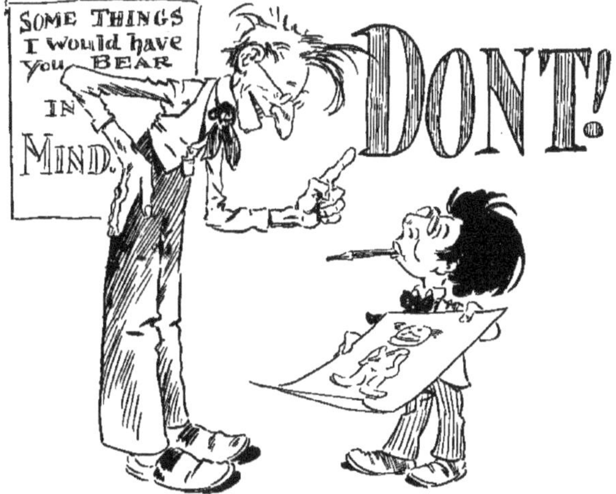

A man, unless he is too vain, likes to be caricatured.

Don't draw things which are liable to reflect unfavorably upon your character.

Ignore questionable subjects; everything lewd or obscene. Good, thinking people—who compose the largest class that enjoy your efforts—despise such work, as well as the artist who produces it.

RIGHT AND WRONG INTERIORS

I GIVE you here two views of an interior, showing the right and wrong way of grouping your furniture and bric-a-brac, so that parallel lines will not conflict with one another.

In another part of this book I have made a sketch of the interior of a grocery store, to demonstrate how the long continuous lines should be broken into by other objects. Now I want to call your attention to the conflicting parallel lines in the sketch No. 1, and the same interior as it should be drawn in sketch No. 2. This does not apply to interiors alone, but in the grouping of human and animal bodies the same rule should be followed.

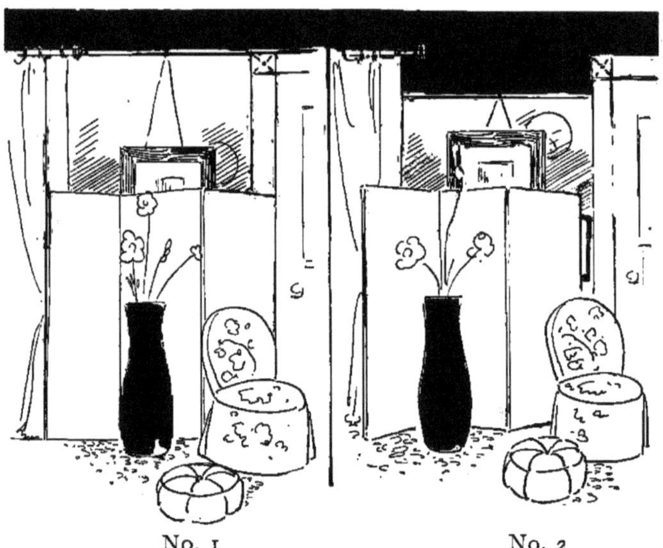

No. 1 No. 2

Don't overcrowd your drawings. Put in just enough to explain the joke, with sufficient details in the background to make the whole tolerable. There is such a thing as being too funny. Like the comedian of the stage, you must know when and where to stop or you will weary your audience.

Don't get offended when anyone feels disposed to criticise your work. Even the criticism of an inexperienced person may put fresh thought into your own brain. The innocent prattle of a child will often give one an idea. The experienced artist welcomes criticism.

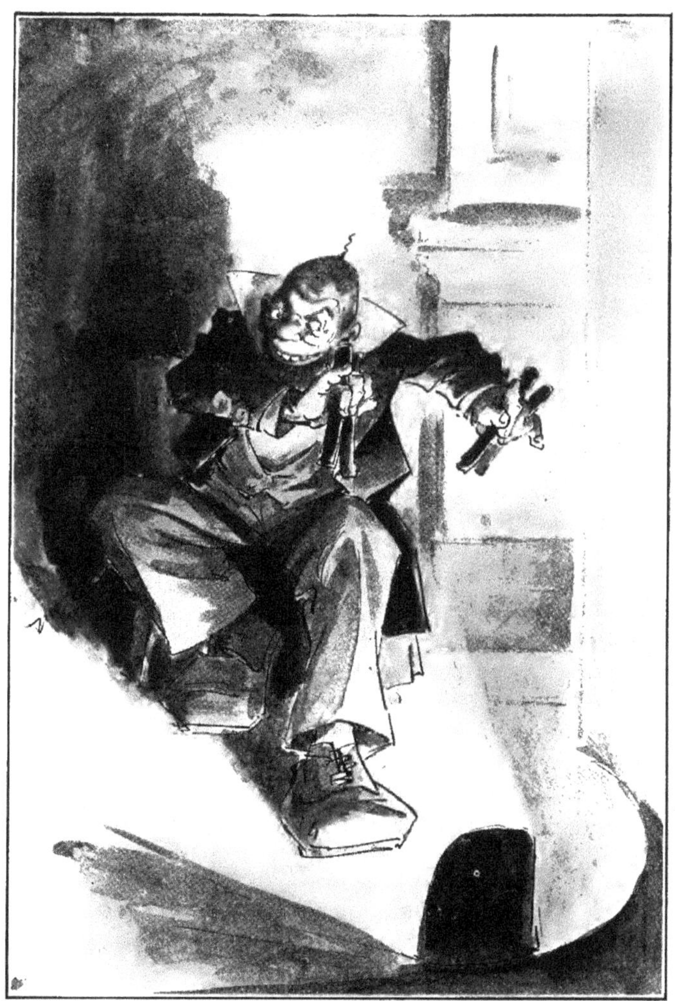

WASH DRAWING

This is termed a wash drawing. First outline your figure lightly, then wash in with water color lamp black made thin with water, the light parts first, gradually making it stronger by working it over until you attain the effect desired. On white cardboard the above result may be accomplished without using white paint, but if made on tinted cardboard you must use white for high lights, the eyes, cuffs and shirt bosom in particular. A soft effect may be had by using slightly tinted gray board, the engraving is called "Half-tone," the process of which I have described in another part of the book.

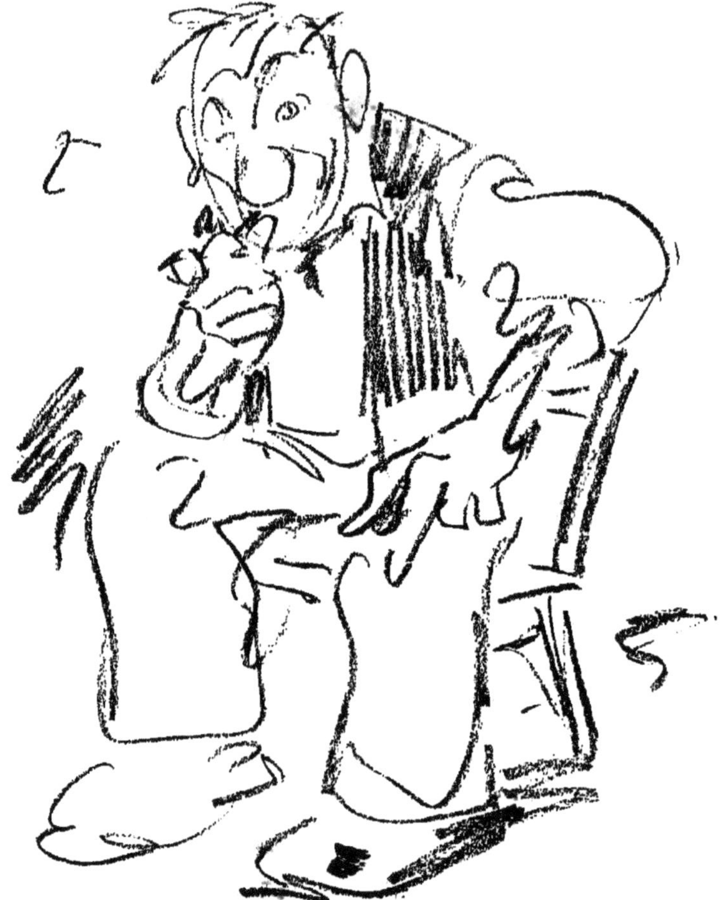

ROUGH PENCIL SKETCH

DOES IT PAY TO BE YOUR OWN PRESS AGENT?

It may not be good taste to blow one's own horn, though all newspapers do it and profit well thereby. Yet how should we ever have been aware that Dr. Kilmer's Swamp Root is such a spring-time marvel, and Lydia Pinkham's concoction would never have been known to the world had not she herself extolled its superior merits, and again we would never have dreamed that No. 23 cures colds and coughs, that No. 13 is good for spine in the back and ingrown

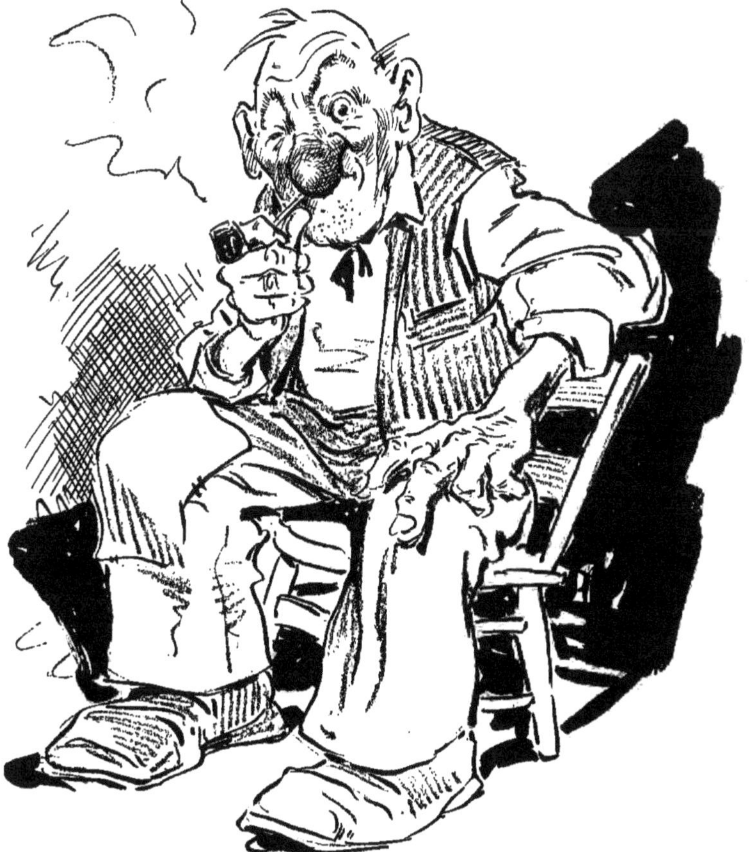

FINISHED DRAWING

toenails were it not for Munyon's own and oft repeated words of assurance that such is the case.

But dare you or I look the public in the face and exclaim, "I am the great and only 57 variety artistic Pickle. With a single dose of my pencil I will change your sad countenance into perpetual giggles." No, indeed, if you did this some uniformed gentleman would bear you to a padded cell and your salary in the outside world would cease. Keep a closed mouth and let the public do the talking. It's a slow process to success, but a sure one if you deserve it.

WHERE NATURE EXCEEDS ART

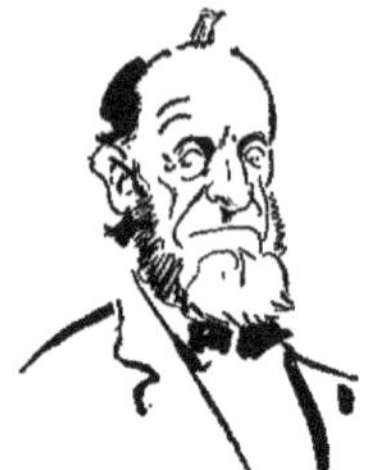

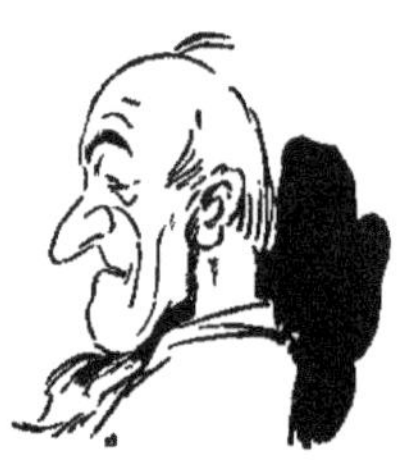

HOW did nature ever think of so many funny things? That is the question you often ask yourself as you look upon some living caricature walking along the streets. Nature has certainly accomplished wonders in that line. She has produed characters that even the cleverest pencil cannot improve upon, so it is wise to stick to nature. Let nature form the basis of all your drawings, then distort it to a limited degree.

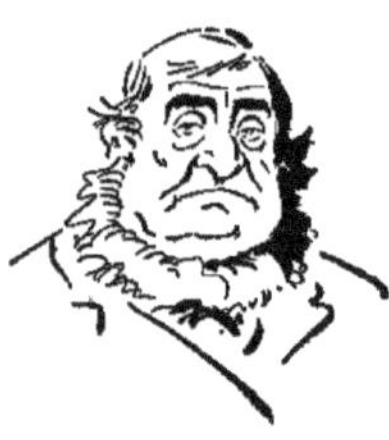

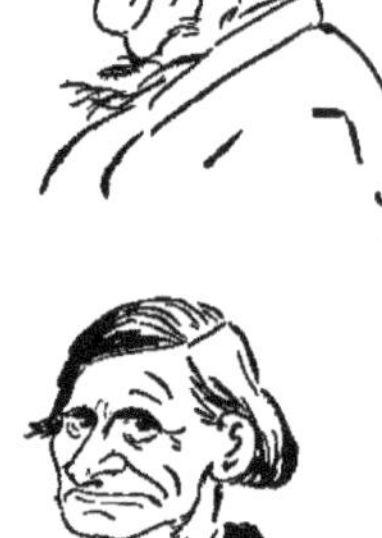

Caricature is nothing more nor less than nature distorted. If you intend to follow the art of caricaturing you had better begin the collecting of photos and prints of public men. You may some day be obliged to use them in your cartoons.

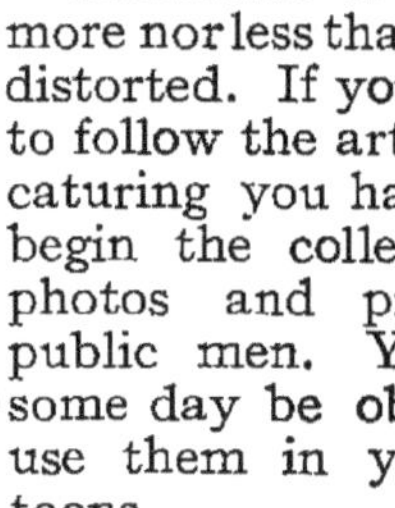

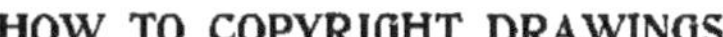

HOW TO COPYRIGHT DRAWINGS

If you invent an idea and wish to retain control over it for the purpose of publishing it yourself you should have it copyrighted. Send to the Librarian of Congress, Washington, D. C., for a copyright application blank, fill it out and send it with a print of your drawing just as it will appear on the market. The cost is slight, not exceeding one dollar. Remit fee with your application.

Do not copyright your work if you wish to sell it to a publisher. The publisher always reserves that right, when he buys your drawing he buys all the privileges that go with it.

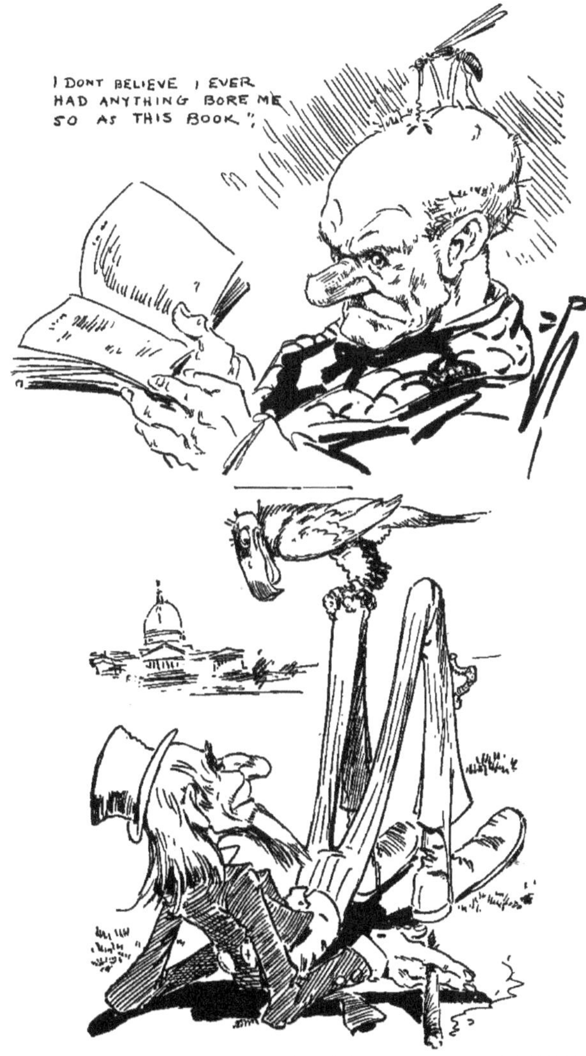

TREATMENT OF SUBJECTS IN PEN AND INK FOR PHOTO-ENGRAVING FOR ORDINARY NEWSPAPER ILLUSTRATION

THE PIRATE

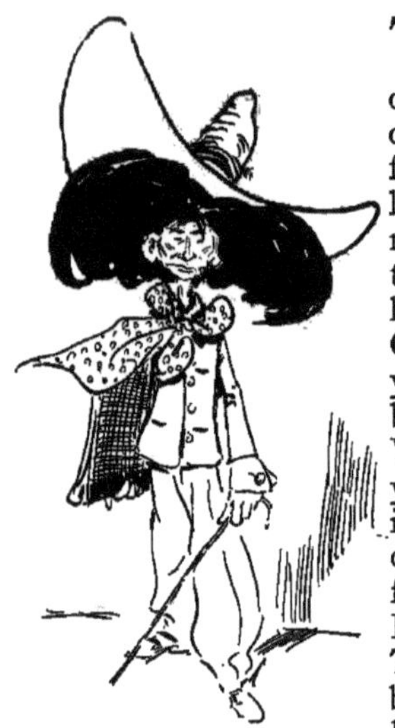

THE man who imitates the work of another and offers it for publication as original is known to the profession as a pirate. The publisher being the first to recognize the imitation, there is a possibility that his work will be rejected. Create a distinct style of your own; you can do this by not imitating others. When you have weaned yourself from the habit of imitating, you will find it quite easy to invent new faces and comic situations. Be original, by all means. The originator is sought by the publisher and receives handsome reward for his productions. The imitator is not so much in demand. Besides, there is a feeling of satisfaction in the knowledge that you have given the public something entirely original, even if it isn't so well executed.

Some artists, in laying out a drawing, will first make an elaborate sketch upon thin Manila paper, then rub upon the reverse side of the Manila paper some powdered Prussian blue, making a tracing paper of it. This done, they trace the drawing upon Bristol board with a steel point or hard pencil, after which the drawing is finished in India ink. This is a slow and tedious method, during which you lose much of the snap and fire of the original sketch. I always draw directly upon the Bristol board with soft pencil, keeping the Bristol board as clean as possible. I do not confine myself closely to the pencil lines, but make any changes with my pen that I find necessary in the completion of my drawing.

POLITICAL CARTOONING

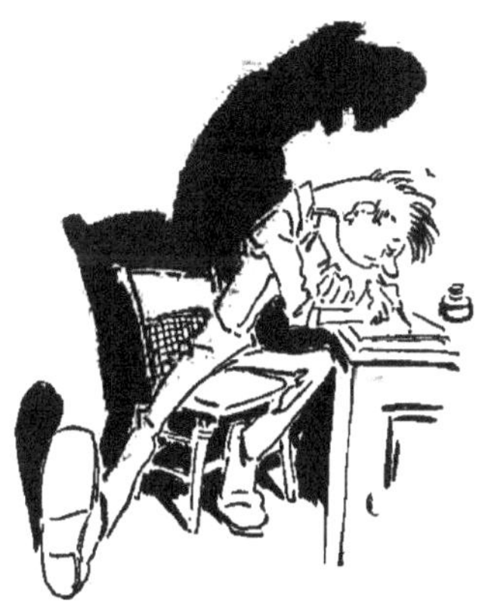

THE caricaturist of to-day who holds a good salaried position has no sinecure. He must represent one or the other of the political elements—shifting from side to side weakens his arguments. He must take up the gauntlet of his chosen party and adhere strictly to its principles. His ideas must be confined to the welfare of the paper that gives him employment as well as his party. He cannot shift about, attacking at random. He must first ascertain if an attack is to the welfare or detriment of his publication, or else he may injure its circulation. He must not create imaginary wrongs, but attack such political dealings as are known facts. With his pencil he must speak the sentiments of the public, not his own entirely. Should the circulation drop off a few thousand copies or gain a few thousand it is liable to be the cause of the cartoon; for naturally a powerful cartoon, such as will cause comment on the street and at the club, or notices to appear in newspapers in its favor, will induce the public to buy the paper, and swell its circulation. For this sort of cartoon the caricaturist is ever on the alert. Freelancing or peddling jokes, sketches and drawings is perhaps the most satisfactory way to begin. It brings the unknown artist to the notice of many publishers of varied tastes.

If your drawings do not suit the fancy of one publisher they may another, and so you will eventually find a publisher who will insist on having a contract with you for your entire product. To my knowledge most of the artists whose names are familiar to us have started in this manner on their professional journey.

While it is generally known that most cartoonists command good salaries, you must not lose sight of the fact that many made martyrs of themselves in the beginning on salaries of five and eight dollars a week—their salaries increasing with long service and popularity of their work.

HISTORY, BIOGRAPHY, FACTS AND FIBS

THE day I began to inflict myself upon the public as a caricaturist was a certain Monday in the fall of 1882—I think it must have been blue Monday—perched upon the tailboard of a Metropolitan street car, with only a friedcake and a cup of weak coffee to bolster up my inner youth and lay the corner-stone for an illustrious career. Yes, it seemed to me the bluest Monday I had ever experienced. Nobody appeared to realize my importance in this world—that a future great man was among them. I was received at the office of a certain weekly publication without the blare of trumpets and booming of cannon, and after the usual preliminaries, I sauntered into the open air to select a cafe befitting my salary and station. Meanwhile, the following inducement, swinging in that blue Monday atmosphere, caught my eager eye:

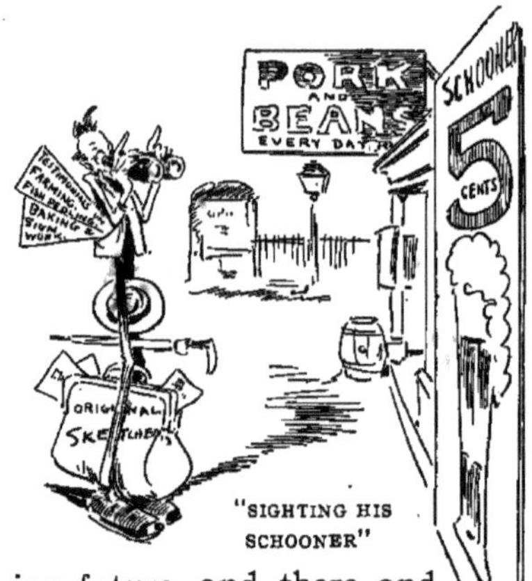

"PORK AND BEANS AND A BIG SCHOONER FOR 5C."

"SIGHTING HIS SCHOONER"

I weighed up the prospects of a glowing future, and there and then did I declare that place my "Delmonico" and for seventeen weeks did I subject myself to the hateful gout. My salary gradually increased, and I was soon able to sit down to Hungarian goulosh and "a la modes" with impunity.

Many would like to live this life over, but I, dear friend, with the memories of that Greenwich Street cafe still fresh in my mind—"Nay! Nay! Pauline!"

Previous to that period my existence was conspicuously uneventful, except that my father never wholloped me in his life, and sometimes would let me sleep in his bake-shop on the tops of flour barrels.

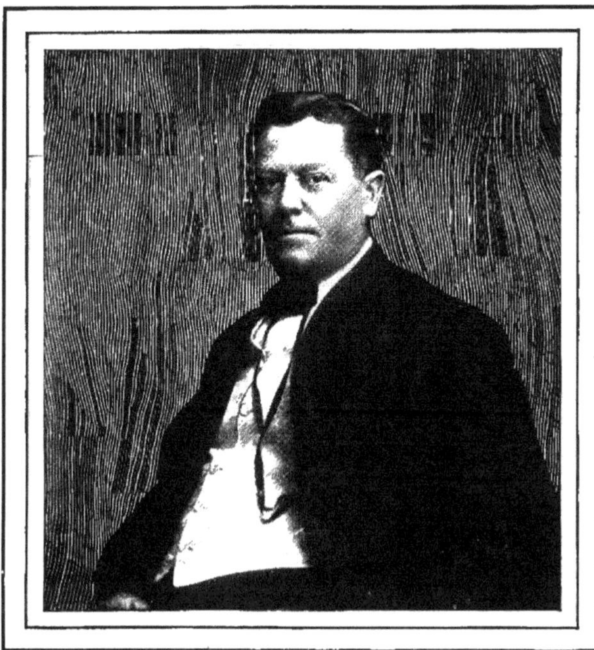

By the time you have reached this the 81st page of this book I think you may think Cartoonists are a funny lot, so I insert here my latest photo by Gessford of N. Y. After all, you see I look very much like any other man who loves his work, and in loving his work, has succeeded in making a place for himself in the world

ZIM

ITHOGRAPHY

PRODUCTION OF COLORED CARTOONS

DOUBLE page (colored) cartoons are drawn upon lithographic stone. This stone is imported and is from 2½ to 4 inches in thickness, has a smooth, light gray surface, slightly grained, so as to take hold of crayon readily. The crayons used for this purpose are of a greasy nature and are graduated: soft, medium and hard.

When the crayon work of the cartoon is finished it is outlined with lithograph ink, also of a greasy nature. This done, the cartoon passes out of the hands of the artist and receives the attention of the transferer. That man puts the stone through a process of acid, after which impression is taken upon starched paper. Duplicates are made upon other stones or metal sheets from the starched sheets of paper.

The original stone is rarely used to print from; it is kept for the purpose of making transfers. Four complete copies of "JUDGE" are printed at one impression on the press. I mean by this that four front pages, four double pages and four back pages are printed at once upon a single sheet of paper, then cut apart, consequently requiring only one-fourth the time to run off the week's edition.

Each additional color, red, blue, gray, yellow, etc., requires separate stones, which also undergo a similar process. This is called Lithography.

YOU CANNOT JUDGE A MAN BY HIS MAKEUP

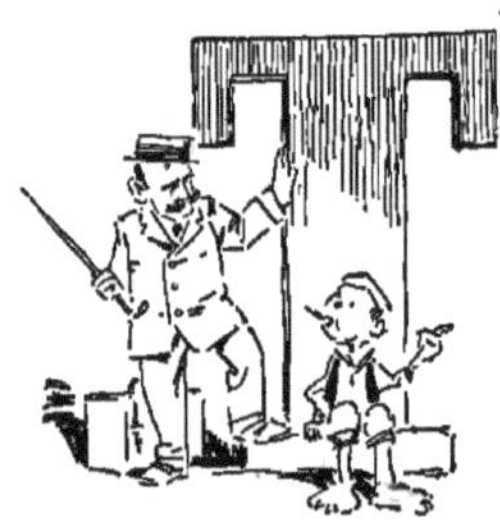

HE following conversation was overheard by a friend, and imparted to me on the quiet, with a bit of advice to change my makeup.

Commercial traveler, approaching tough kid—"Say, bub, ain't that lean fellow with black, curly hair over on the corner 'Whats-his-name,' the artist?"

"Naw, dat's the deputy sheriff, de chief of police, first assistant of de fire department, etcetra, he tends bar in his fadder's hotel. But yer see dat feller over on der udder corner, wid a red nose and looks like a cider bar'l? Well, he's de feller what youse tought de udder was."

AMERICAN CARICATURE'S FOUNDER

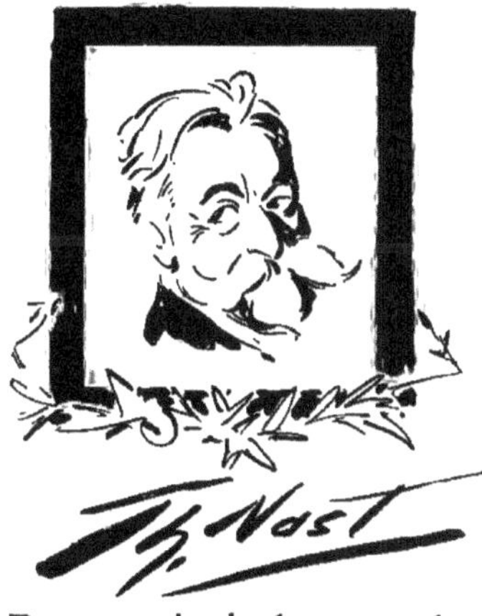

WHENEVER we speak of caricature it is quite natural to drift back some forty or fifty years to the real beginning of the era of American caricature and its founder, Thos. Nast.

Thos. Nast was a potent factor in directing public opinion against the political thieves of that period. Nast was original. It was he who originated the Republican elephant, and the Democratic jackass, each respectively symbolical of its party. Now, if Nast's political principles had been Democratic and his drawings published by a Democratic paper, he might have created the jackass as the symbol of the hateful Republican party, and the elephant might have been used to typify the sentiment of the Grand Old Democracy.

Nast had an odd technic; unlike anything of the present day, a style which was hard to imitate. His faces were excellent specimens of caricature. Although you will hardly find an imitator of the Nast style, his name will live for centuries.

In Nast's day public attention was centered to one paper, HARPER'S WEEKLY, to see what Nast had to say. It was an era of terrible political corruption. He had abundance of material at hand, a powerful paper to put it forward, and no rivalry to impede his fearless onslaughts.

He stood conspicuously alone in the field of caricature. At the present time there are hundreds of caricaturists on the various daily and weekly papers, who, under similar circumstances, would be considered just as clever as was Thos. Nast; but such advantages as he enjoyed are things of the past. We honor his memory, nevertheless, for setting us the pace.

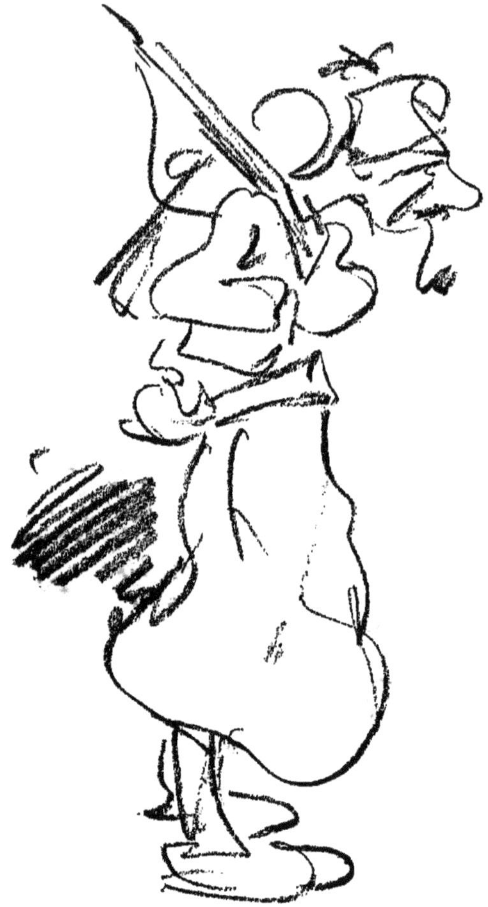

PENCIL SKETCH

This is a rough pencil sketch "hot off the bat," as Dooley might say, dashed off just as the idea struck me. It might appear to be a careless roughout but look it over, there's a lesson to be learnt from it.

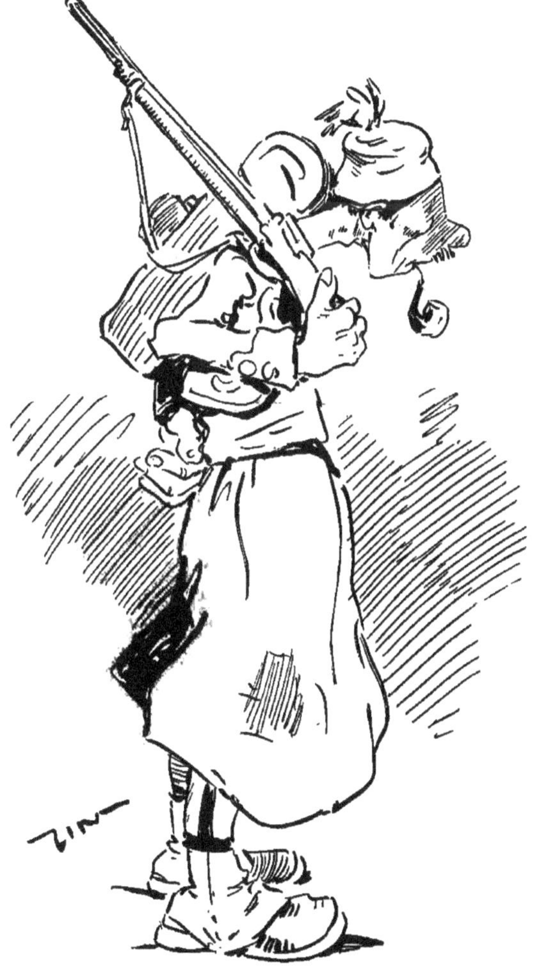

FINISHED DRAWING

This is a more or less finished pen sketch worked up from the drawing on the opposite page. You will notice that I do not adhere strictly to my original lay-out, no artist really does.

A LITTLE ABOUT THE EAR!

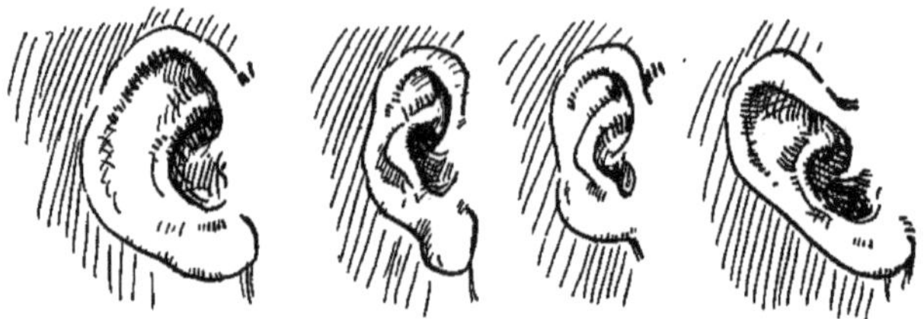

A LITTLE ABOUT THE EAR.

THE EAR AND ITS RELATION TO THE FACE

WHEN we caricature a prominent individual we lay great stress on portraying the general features, such as the eyes, nose and mouth, but seldom do we give the proper attention to drawing the ears Ears are not all alike, each human face has its characteristic ears. No other ears will fit that particular face and resemble the original.

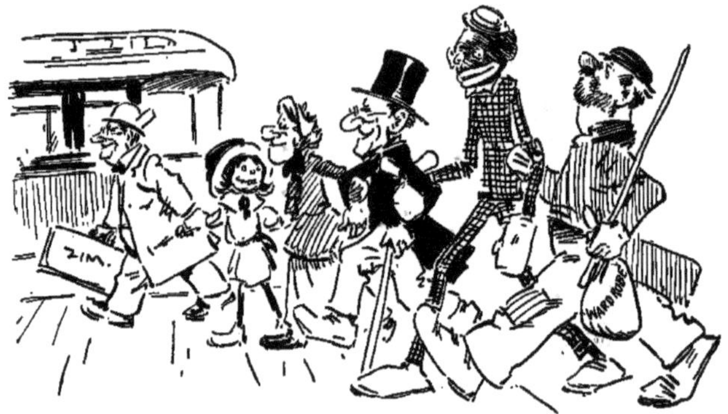

REGARDING BLACKS AND WHITES

I once received a telegram from the Art Editor of our paper asking me to come to New York at once and bring along all the black and whites I could scrape together. Of course he meant black and white drawings for the inside of the paper; but the inquisitive depot operator placed a different construction to it. So he noised it about that I was getting up an excursion for the poor Blacks and Whites of the town and he had the station agent quote me special rates on parties of from twenty-five to solid vestibule train loads.

I hope with the advent of a universal language, technical terms will be abolished.

(See page 54)

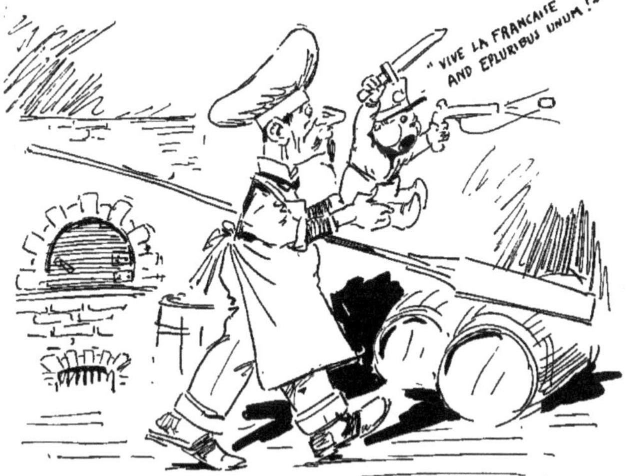

"I IMPLORED HIM TO TAKE ME TO THE FRONT."

ONE SIDED HUMOR

WHEN the Boer war was at its zenith an English acquaintance remarked that there was the opportunity of a lifetime for the comic artist to depict funny incidents. "I cannot see," said I, "that there in anything particularly mirthful in the slaughter and slashing of good and true men." "Why, just think of the many funny attitudes of the Englishmen jabbing bayonets through the stomachs of the horrid Boers," said my acquaintance.

"Now," said I, "let us take the opposite view, let us vice-versa this thing which strikes you as being so extremely funny. Suppose we make the Boers jumping into the air and jabbing bayonets through the well-filled stomachs of the English, would it still appeal to you in the same light?"

"Oh, mercy, no! That would be simply horrible indeed."

That goes to show that one-sided humor which causes joy to one and pain to another is not the popular brand.

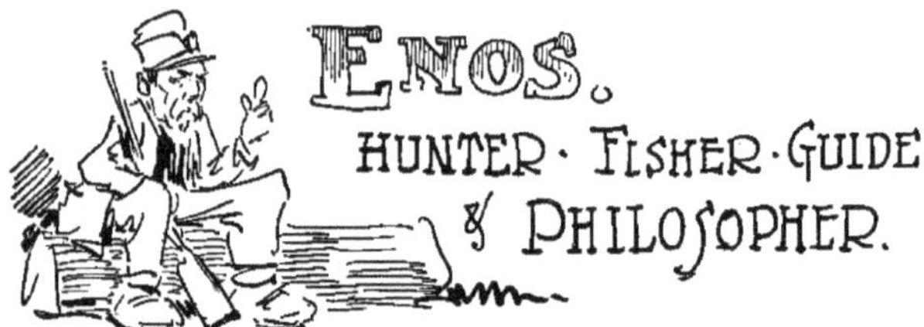

DURING my early days, when my artistic struggles were discouragingly hard, I found myself in a broken-down condition. I forthwith made the acquaintance of a modern nimrod by the name of Ene. This old man's easy going disposition seemed to soothe my nerves to sleep. I traveled about with him almost constantly.

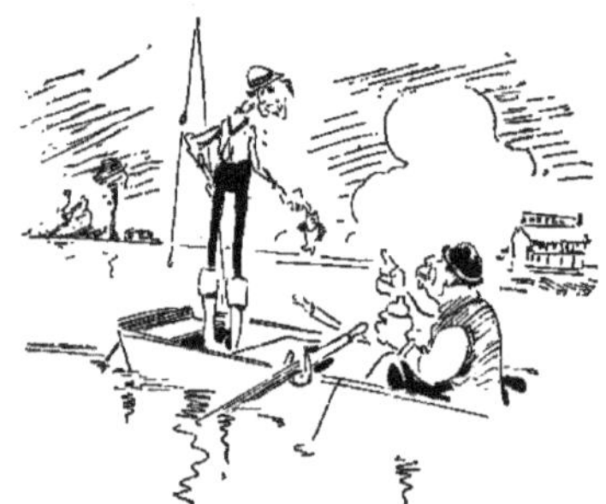

He had a language of his own make. His vocabulary fairly sparkled with quaint profanity. But he was a fine character in himself, and above all he was no fool, as I soon found out. Our wanderings led us along streams and through woodlands where he would describe to me the habits of fish and game and explain the various methods of trapping and snaring, point out tracks and other indications of game so that I was soon able to distinguish one track from another. What I learned from this man has benefited me in depicting sporting life, from the true sport to the pot hunter.

I quote here a few of his own manufactured sentences of wisdom, which were uttered with great seriousness and oratorical splendor. Ene, after regarding a bass I had hauled in and commented on its diminutive proportions

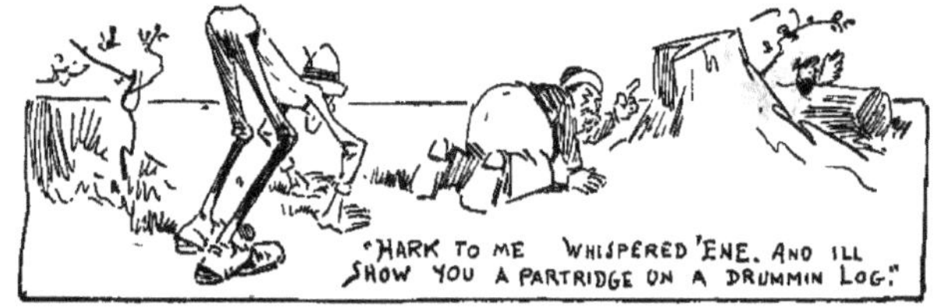

said, in an effort to console me, "Why, say, Bubby, I'd rather have a bass o' that size accordingly, than to have one larger of the same proportions."

Then again, when I happened to pay a tribute to quail on toast for a sick stomach, he answered, "Wild game!

Why, it's the best meat they is for a sick man, 'cause it substitutes on the plantation of this earth."

He taught me also how to set a "dead fall" for skunks, how to find ginseng, a root valuable for medical purposes, and decidedly rare in its wild state; how to distinguish sassafras from other herbs, etc.

He was known as just plain "En," or "Enos" in the community, an honest citizen, a battle-scarred veteran, living largely on his well-earned pension and the proceeds from the services rendered as guide and companion. I attribute much of my present good health, and in a measure, my success to this very man, for with his simple philosophy he put me back into working order, besides giving me the sort of natural schooling I most needed in my business.

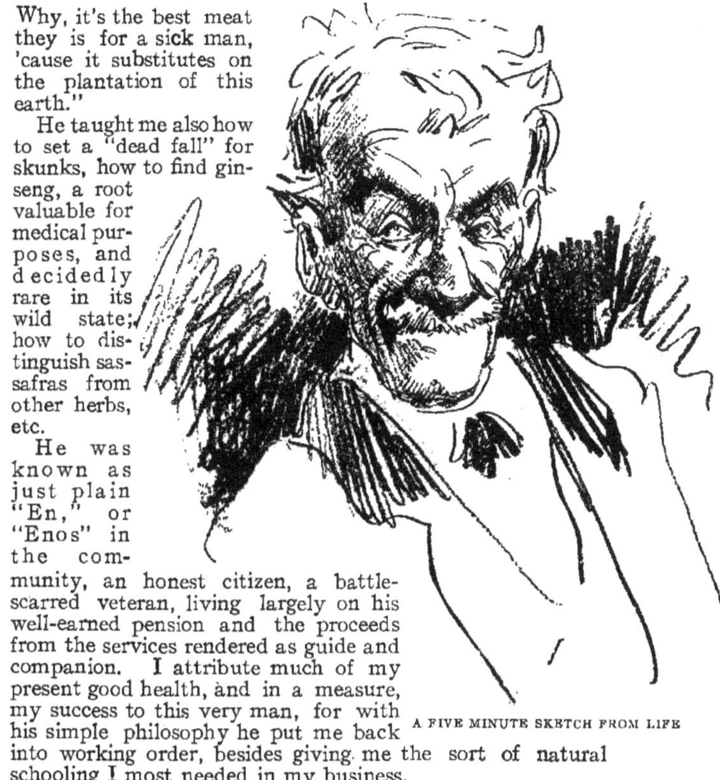

A FIVE MINUTE SKETCH FROM LIFE

PONDERING OVER THE PAST

Sometimes we sit and ponder over the past. The many side steps taken in early life, which were merely circumstantial by-plays, because of that great obstacle, necessity, that stood in our way and impeded our progress straightway. Perhaps these very moves were responsible for the success we attained.

There is little satisfaction in having your course laid in advance, someone to blaze the way for you. Better an encouraging slap on the back than a bank roll. The money is liable to make you lazy. The slap on the back will make you determined to show what's in you.

Gather in all the knowledge you can as you journey along, but in the main make your success your own success, made strictly by yourself.

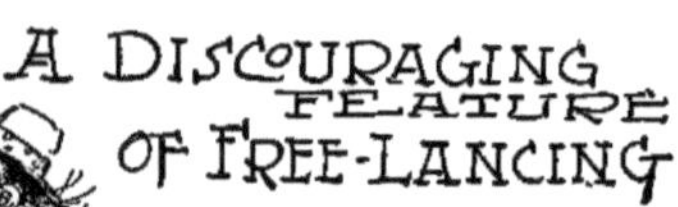

An artist enters a publishing house to submit what he deems his very best effort, he is cordially invited to remain outside of railing number one, while the janitor or the high-salaried office boy escorts said wonderful production into the Editor of the Art Department. Said Editor of said Art Department is usually a large unsympathetic man, or perhaps a slender man of bilious mien. Invariably the art editor is too busy to give the matter immediate attention, so the parcel or package is consigned to a receptacle for that purpose, in one corner, there to repose until Wednesday next at 2 P. M. News to that effect is conveyed to the art gentleman in waiting, that on the following Wednesday a letter would be forthcoming advising him of the art editor's investigations and decision in the matter. Meanwhile the art gentlemen pays homage to free lunches and argues in his mind whether he shall dine at Rector's, Beaux Arts or the Waldorf the following Wednesday.

On Wednesday precisely at 2 P. M., providing the U. S. mail is in normal condition, he receives the long-coveted letter which informs him by way of an insignificant card printed in common type and plain black, something like this:

> We regret to say your drawings are not available. Kindly send in some more.
>
> THE ART EDITOR.

The professional is accustomed and hardened to this sort of treatment, but the novice is liable to become discouraged and drop out of the game. That is what is termed "Free-lancing."

MORAL

Better you look corned beef hash in the face immediately than live in constant expectation of a warm bird and a cold bottle.

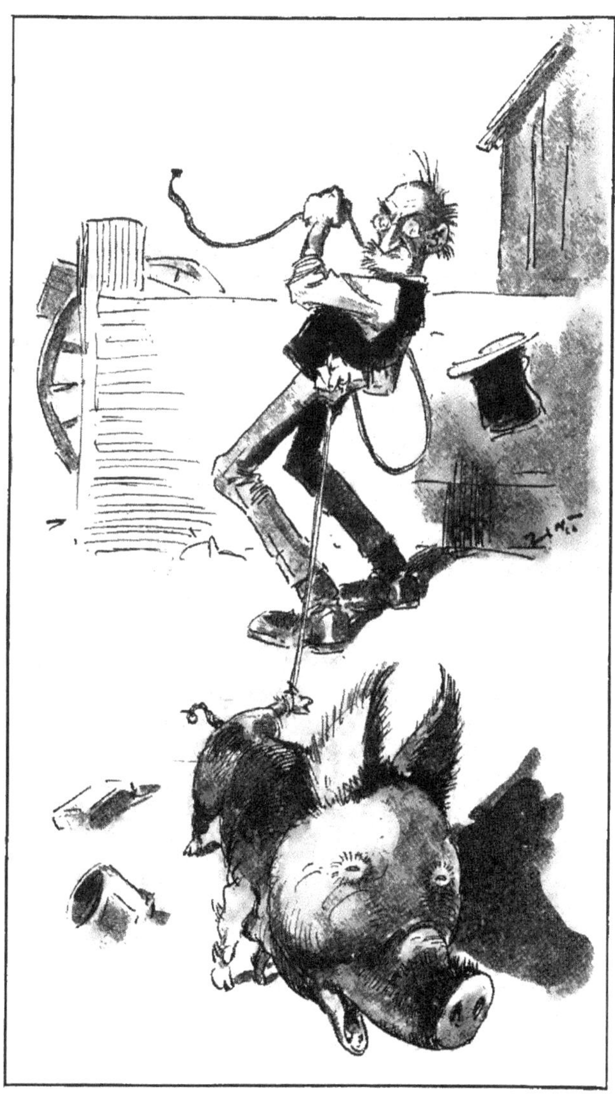

Truly, this is a contrary world!

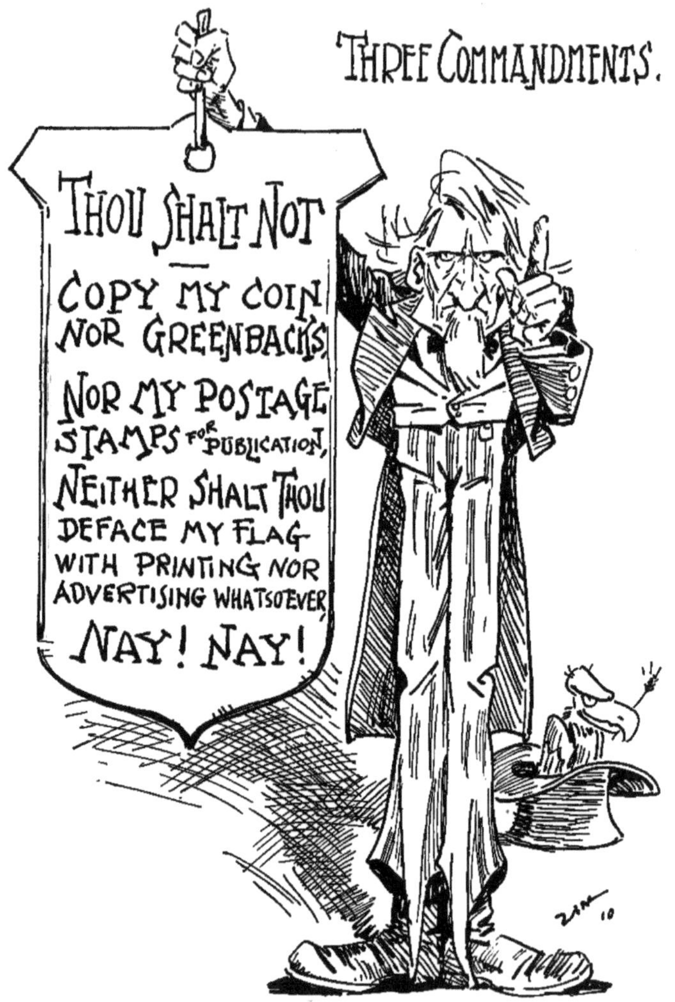

HIS, COMMANDMENT

OLD UNCLE SAM is an awful funny fellow and easy to get along with so long as you pay attention to his rules and regulations, but if you get gay and step on his corns, gee whiz!! no telling what'll happen to you, so you'd better do just as he tells you, and mebbe save a heap o' trouble.

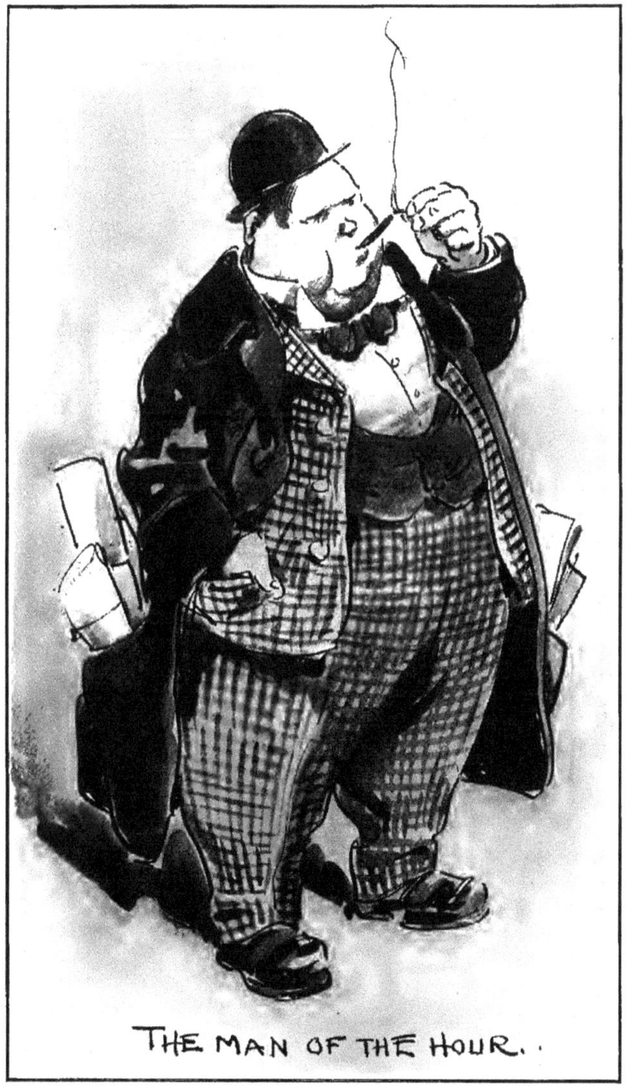

THE MAN OF THE HOUR. .

"I want to leave some of my 'stuff' with you. The gags are written on the back. If you don't find anything to suit you among this bunch, throw them in the waste basket and I'll fetch in some more."

This is the sort of a comic artist that is never without work and at a high market price.

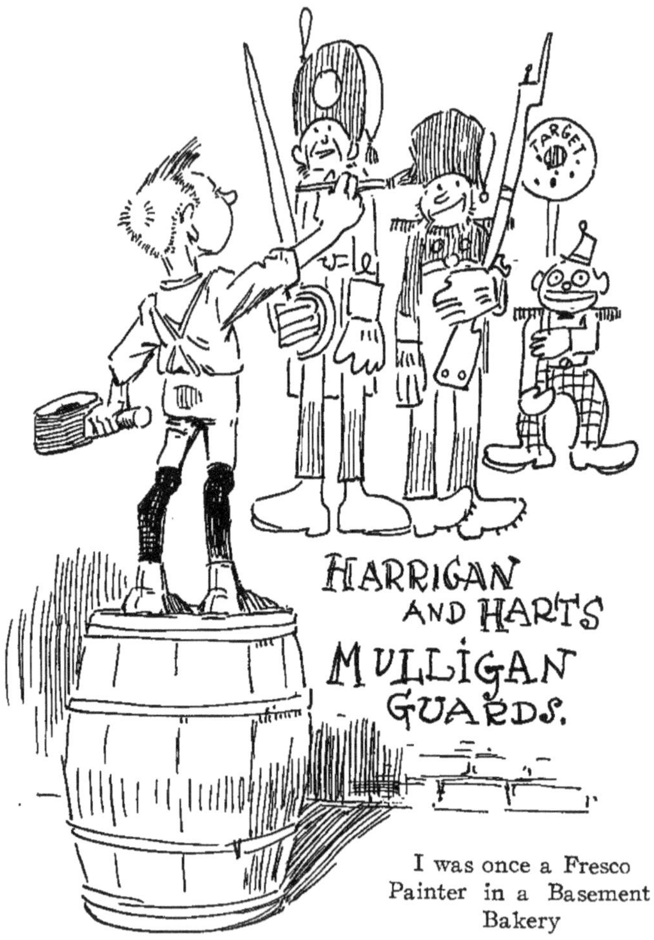

I was once a Fresco Painter in a Basement Bakery

IN the eyes of the owner of the bake shop and others equally eminent and able to judge, this was the first great work of my life. A colossal fresco in lamp black and kerosene oil upon a whitewashed wall near the hot oven. It earned for me my release from the calling which I so handsomely detested, and shortly thereafter I went into farming business.

ODD REMARKS BY AN ODD FELLOW

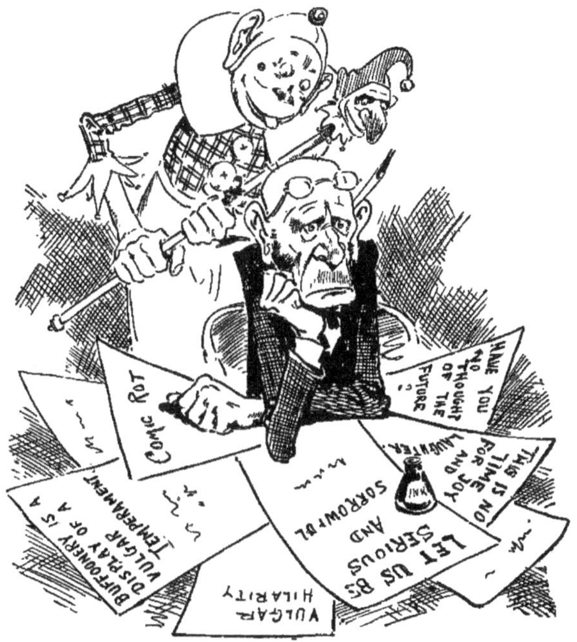

THE most pitiful object on earth is the man whose ideas of humor are so narrow that he looks with scorn upon joking in any form—he who calls it undignified or vulgar to cause the cracking of a smile. His cup of joy was soured at his birth, perhaps, and he cannot help his natural condition. At any rate let him alone—don't try to sweeten his existence with your own gifts of nature. Keep busy. "The men who are busy miss half of the woe that's hunting for victims to slay; they get all the cream in this valley below, while idlers subsist on the whey; while Fortune kicks others she'll give you a kiss, you'll win more applause, and you'll know more of bliss if you always keep pegging away."

With these remarks I close my book.

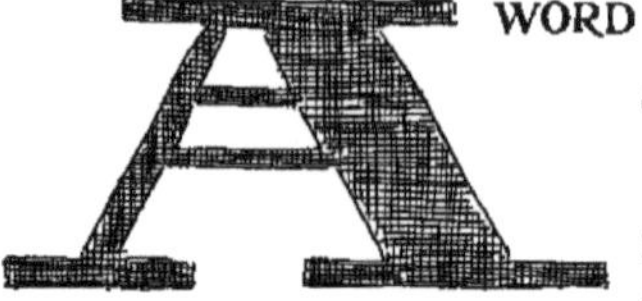

WORD BEFORE CLOSING

THE author wishes to state that no effort has been made at caricaturing himself in the foregoing sketches. His wish is merely to depict a type of the ideal or imaginary comic artist.

The matter for this book was compiled while the author was down with the measles. Having much time on his hands and pimples upon his person at that time, he feels justified in referring to it as a measley book; however, it has nothing but new and original material within its covers. Not even the paper, nor printer's ink has ever before been used, and as the proofreader insisted upon a third reading before publication, the author feels safe in recommending it to the afflicted.

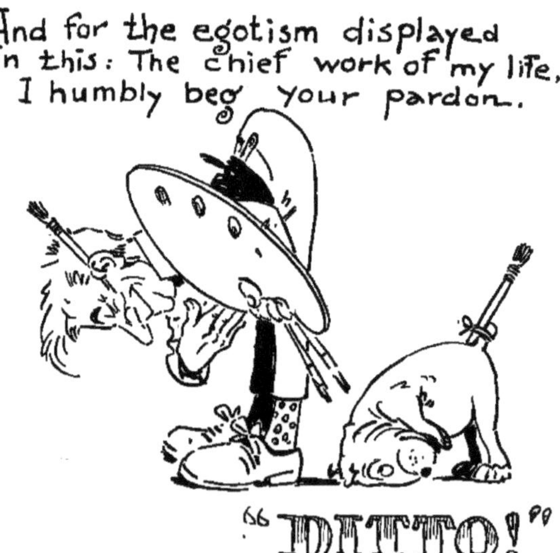

More Zim books from
New York History Review
by Eugene Zimmerman

Zim's Foolish History of Elmira

Zim's Foolish History of Horseheads

In Dairyland

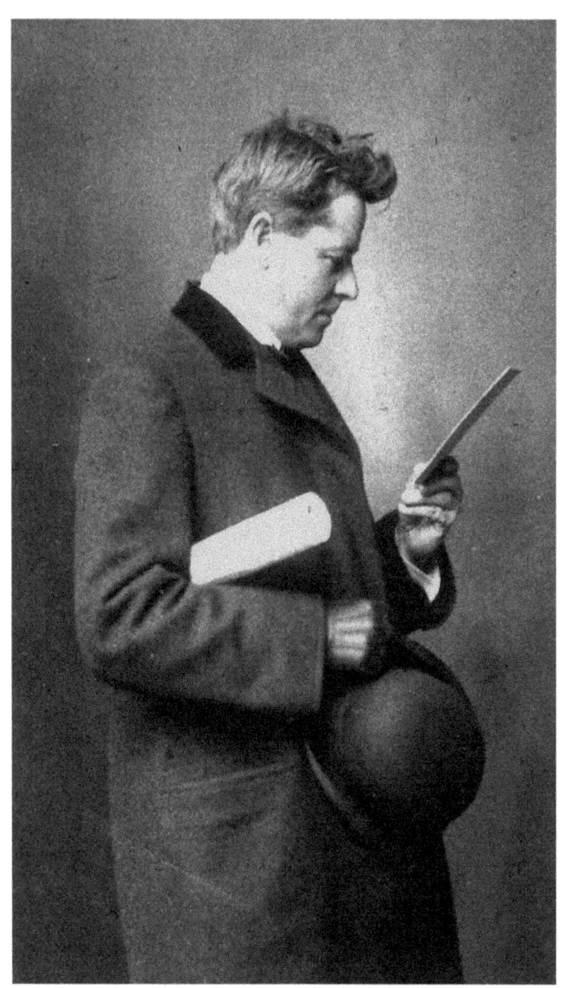

Eugene Zimmerman, circa 1886.

Eugene Zimmerman was born in Basel, Switzerland. After his mother died he was sent to live with relatives in Alsace. In 1867 his father, who was a baker, and an older brother emigrated to the United States. In 1868 Zimmerman was placed on a ship and followed them.

Poverty and restricted circumstances characterized his early years as he moved from relatives to working in different jobs. In 1877 he became an apprentice sign painter and continued in this line of work for several years, nurturing a desire to become a professional cartoonist. By copying the work of cartoonists, he acquired the skills necessary to gather a portfolio, which gained him an interview in May 1883 with *Puck* magazine. He was hired and began work at one of the most remarkable satirical magazines of the late 19th century. While he worked at Puck, he supplemented his income with lucrative freelance work. In 1885 he dropped the last portion of his signature and became known as Zim.

After two and a half years at *Puck* (from May 1883 to December 1885), Zim moved to *Judge* magazine, The following year he married Mabel Alice Beard of Horseheads, New York. In 1888, he and Mabel moved to Horseheads. Zim then traveled to New York on alternate weeks to fulfill his commitments at the magazine. Like many contemporary cartoonists, Zim generated cartoons of all varieties, including some which could be considered offensive for their ethnic stereotypes. He remained at *Judge* until his retirement in 1912.

Zim published more than 40,000 sketches in his lifetime. After his retirement from Judge, Zim was founder and first president of the American Association of Cartoonists and Caricaturists.

He died on March 26, 1935.

www.ingramcontent.com/pod-product-compliance
Lightning Source LLC
LaVergne TN
LVHW052347100826
845147LV00012B/775

* 9 7 8 1 9 5 0 8 2 2 2 5 6 *